One Proposal

Dalia Franco
Michelle Burzynski, Editor

Copyright © 2017 Dalia Franco
All rights reserved
Printed in the United States of America

Published by Author Academy Elite
P.O. Box 43, Powell, OH 43035
www.AuthorAcademyElite.com

All rights reserved. No part of this publication may be reproduced, stored in a retrieval system, or transmitted in any form or by any means—for example, electronic, photocopy, recording—without the prior written permission of the publisher. The only exception is brief quotations in printed reviews.

Paperback ISBN: 978-1-946114-61-7
Hardcover ISBN: 978-1-946114-60-0

Library of Congress Control Number: 2017938195

Scripture quotations marked ESV are from The ESV® Bible (The Holy Bible, English Standard Version®), copyright © 2001 by Crossway, a publishing ministry of Good News Publishers. Used by permission. All rights reserved

Scripture quotations marked (NIV) are taken from the Holy Bible, New International Version®, NIV®. Copyright © 1973, 1978, 1984, 2011 by Biblica, Inc.™ Used by permission of Zondervan. All rights reserved worldwide. www.zondervan.com The "NIV" and "New International Version" are trademarks registered in the United States Patent and Trademark Office by Biblica, Inc.™

Scripture quotations marked (AMP) are taken from the Amplified Bible, Copyright © 1954, 1958, 1962, 1964, 1965, 1987 by The Lockman Foundation. Used by permission.

Scripture quotations taken from the Amplified® Bible (AMPC),
Copyright © 1954, 1958, 1962, 1964, 1965, 1987 by The Lockman Foundation
Used by permission. www.Lockman.org"

Scriptures marked NAS are taken from the NEW AMERICAN STANDARD (NAS): Scripture taken from the NEW AMERICAN STANDARD BIBLE®, copyright© 1960, 1962, 1963, 1968, 1971, 1972, 1973, 1975, 1977, 1995 by The Lockman Foundation. Used by permission.

Scriptures marked KJV are taken from the KING JAMES VERSION (KJV): KING JAMES VERSION, public domain.

Scripture quotations marked MSG are taken from THE MESSAGE, copyright © 1993, 1994, 1995, 1996, 2000, 2001, 2002 by Eugene H. Peterson. Used by permission of NavPress. All rights reserved. Represented by Tyndale House Publishers, Inc.

Scripture quotations are taken from the Holy Bible, New Living Translation, copyright ©1996, 2004, 2007, 2013, 2015 by Tyndale House Foundation. Used by permission of Tyndale House Publishers, Inc., Carol Stream, Illinois 60188. All rights reserved.

GOD'S WORD is a copyrighted work of God's Word to the Nations. Quotations are used by permission. Copyright 1995 by God's Word to the Nations. All rights reserved.

Scripture taken from the Holy Bible: International Standard Version®. Copyright © 1996-forever by The ISV Foundation. ALL RIGHTS RESERVED INTERNATIONALLY. Used by permission.

The Holy Bible, Berean Study Bible, BSB
Copyright ©2016 by Bible Hub
Used by Permission. All Rights Reserved Worldwide.

To Him whom my soul loves...

Contents

1	*Facts vs. Truth*	31	*Take This Life*
2	*Still Single*	32	*May I Have This Dance?*
3	*The Old Me*	33	*Mountain Biking*
4	*The Great Escape*	34	*First-Class*
5	*Accepting Jesus*	35	*The Ebb & Flow*
6	*Relationship Goals*	36	*Playing Offense*
7	*Full Potential*	37	*A Word From God*
8	*Me, Myself & I*	38	*What'd He Say?*
9	*Holding Out*	39	*Farmers*
10	*What's Wrong With Me?*	40	*Letting My Guard Down*
11	*Soul-Ties*	41	*Through the Valley…*
12	*Playing Catch-up*	42	*Treasures Untold*
13	*Gut Check*	43	*Silencing the Enemy*
14	*"Cómo estás?"*	44	*Una Sola Hoja*
15	*My Dream Man*	45	*Mind, Will, and Emotions*
16	*Word = Seed*	46	*Conversing with God*
17	*Coincidence? I Think Not*	47	*Wait Training*
18	*It Is Written*	48	*The Greatest Commandment*
19	*It's all Eve's Fault!*	49	*Third Time's a Charm*
20	*Give a Little: Take a Lot*	50	*Self-Made*
21	*Sticks and Stones Never Broke My Bones*	51	*Fairytales*
22	*Boundaries*	52	*Giddy-up!*
23	*In the Driver's Seat*	53	*Remnants*
24	*Scars*	54	*The Other Woman*
25	*Wisdom*	55	*"Just Friends"*
26	*Just as I Am*	56	*Broken Pieces*
27	*Fine-Tuning*	57	*The Significantly Insignificant*
28	*Rejection…Again…*	58	*The Package Deal*
29	*The Good, The Bad and The Ugly*	59	*The Book of Life*
30	*The World Got a Hold of Me First*	60	*The Title One Proposal*

ACKNOWLEDGMENTS

Michelle Burzynski, Editor

…was the one who encouraged me to get my vertical alignment with God right first, before I did anything horizontally, where romantic relationships were concerned many years ago.

Thank you for the investment of your time and dedication to this book. I am eternally grateful that you said yes to this project! Thank you for taking it on as if it were your own. The sweetest words I heard you utter during this entire process were when you referred to the project as *'ours'*. You went above and beyond – doing it all with exceptionally great and meticulous detail. Staying up late - countless hours, thinking about it when you didn't have to…when I asked you months into the process why you said yes to helping me with this book expecting nothing, your answer was 'because you asked'. Thank you for being such a giver of your time and life and doing it with excellence. Michelle, I would not have wanted to do this without you.

Kary Oberbrunner, Coach

Thank you for believing in me and my message when I first spoke to you about the concept of this book. Your support was invaluable when I didn't yet have the clarity I do today. I am extremely thankful for the patience, support and willingness to help you demonstrated me during this entire time. Kary, I could not have done this without you.

Foreword

I don't believe in coincidences. I believe you holding this book is providential.

We live in a time where finding someone to date has become increasingly easy due to technology, yet devastatingly difficult due to a number of other factors. As a former pastor, I saw many women who struggled with being single, thinking that their answer lay in finding "the one." Their entire focus became about finding the one—and in many cases these pursuits never ended happily ever after.

The only thing I have truly found to be life-changing is studying God's Word—and Dalia so beautifully illustrates this in *One Proposal*. If you unpack her stories and explore the Scriptures she outlines, I believe you'll experience significant transformation.

We have an epic opportunity for single women of faith to walk out the plan and purpose for which God created them, first as an individual, and then as a mate.

I invite you to be part of this movement. I pray that you open your heart, renew your mind, and partner with God as you walk into your greatest love story while you wait on the one to marry.

Kary Oberbrunner
Author of *ELIXIR PROJECT*, *Day Job to Dream Job*, *The Deeper Path*, and *Your Secret Name*

"My Lord God, I have no idea where I am going...
I do not see the road ahead of me...
I cannot know for certain where it will end...
Nor do I really know myself, and the fact that I think
I am following Your will does not mean that I am actually doing so."

– Author Unknown

I have lived this faith life quietly, guarding the mention of Jesus on my lips, limiting it to a church building and close friends, seeking after a God I couldn't see or hear, hanging onto the unseen for my very life. I struggled, I doubted, I wept, all in the chaotic confinement of my mind. But today, I sense that He is asking me to open up a very personal area of my life that I have guarded *so* well for *so* long. I am taking the road less traveled, truly believing that the gentle voice tugging on my heart, guiding me on a path I would have never chosen as my own, will lead me safely and purposefully to the One.

As you walk with me through these days ahead, I hope that you find something familiar, something new, a borrowed thought process from a place once very blue. Read one page a day and look up the scriptures outlined at the bottom in your Bible app. Meditate on them; turn them back and forth in your mind, read them out loud, look at each word that makes up that scripture. You haven't finished a page until you've done this, because this is not just a book of stories to relate to, it's about what God is trying to say to you.

Here's to falling in love. Here's to believing in an unseen God for an area of such raging desire. Here's to following His leading, His guidance, trusting that this life of faith I have quietly lived thus far will encourage you to begin your own journey of believing in the faithfulness of God and His Word. As you continue, somewhere beneath the layers of doubt and unbelief – if you just keep digging – lay truth, treasures, and great love.

This is the beginning of my love story...

*Those who sow in tears
shall reap
with shouts of joy!*

Psalm 126:5 ESV

Facts vs. Truth

I wept bitterly. Muffling my uncontrollable sobbing with the running water from the shower, I gave way and collapsed onto the tiled restroom floor, clutching my chest, my lungs gasping for air between each sob. All six of my siblings were just in the next room. The recent holidays (Thanksgiving, Christmas, New Years and Valentines Day) were all spent single – yet again – and on this particular day I was a few weeks shy of adding yet another year to my thirties.

The turn of each New Year marked the renewal of my resolution that this would be the year my most fervent desire would come to pass. My spirit would start strong and resolute. Hope seemed to gain momentum as God spoke to me about this man, but here I was again, tormented in my soul by having yet another year pass with no husband.

I was mourning over the circumstantial facts of the situation. As a woman I should have already gotten married according to the standards of society and my culture. The pool of eligible men was shrinking. Women in their thirties would have a difficult time conceiving a child and have increased pregnancy risks. Men wanted young twenty-something year olds. All the men around my age had already been taken. Besides, we women in our thirties have impossibly high standards. Is there something wrong with us?

But the TRUTH of the matter is in direct opposition to these facts. I am trusting in *the Lord*. God has NOT forgotten me. God can make up the years the locusts ate. He can redeem all matters of time. Though it tarry, wait for it. God strengthens my ability to handle difficulties. God will give me an expected end. God will give me the desires of my heart.

My flesh was weeping. My soul was tormented. But now, my spirit is hopeful.

Habakkuk 3:17-19 AMP
Psalm 27:14 AMPC
Habakkuk 2:3 AMP

Trust in the Lord with all your heart...

Proverbs 3:5 NIV

"...if I don't quit, if I don't give up my life will take a 180° turn... Deep within this hurt I desperately want that change. I have answered this faint, yet persistent knock that was always at the door of my heart..." – Journal Entry, 2008

Truth be told, I never would have imagined that this faith walk would be so difficult, and I never expected to still be single in my thirties. About six years ago, I made a comment to one of my brothers that sounded like I was trying to be really spiritual, but deep within my soul, I really believed the statement I made. I told him that my whole life would be one of faith, *even* where my husband was concerned. I didn't fully understand the declaration I made, but since those words escaped my mouth I have done everything – I have asked, I have prayed, I have begged, I have thanked, I have petitioned, and I have sobbed with such raw emotion to God for this area of my life, and yet, I am still single.

And here's the crazy thing: I am *still* holding out for God to come through. To family and friends, and the rest of the world, it seems like I'm doing nothing. I don't date around anymore, I don't go out of my way to make myself seen by men, I don't chase after guys, I don't do the online dating thing. Instead, I am still seeking, pursuing, thanking, and believing God for this area of my life.

I want what *the Word* says I can have, even while, to so many others, my stance seems foolish. I am not backing down, even as my biological clock continues ticking. I am not giving up. I can't give up. There's no turning back. I want God's best for my life and nothing less.

Isaiah 30:18 MSG
Proverbs 3:5-6 AMPC
2 Chronicles 15:1-9 GWT

Man looks at the outward appearance, but God looks at the heart...

1 Samuel 16:7 NAS

The Old Me

"I went out last night with a group, making small talk with a co-worker's girlfriend... I mentioned I was interested in a certain guy who is involved in politics. She said I should look for someone who is more "attainable", someone who is on the same "level" and "rank" as me... Lord, I felt stupid – is that how people see me?" – Journal Entry, 2004

I hated the person I was – I really did. I hid behind a façade of smiles and nods. I was afraid of being found out how dumb I really was. I didn't talk much or share my opinions *ever*. I was never quick enough to put together the right words in my head and articulate them from my mouth. So when this individual expressed my deepest fear, it sent me diving further into the abyss of self-loathing and self-pity.

I didn't have the looks, didn't have the money, nor the clothes, no position, no education. Having lived a very sheltered life, I didn't know about clothing trends or current events. I especially hated that I was so skinny and scrawny, feeling like a walking toothpick with a bushel of excessively thick hair since childhood. I wasn't capable of holding an intelligent conversation, just always fixated on how stupid I would sound, cringing inside at the very thought of being found out. So, I said nothing.

Everything that the world deemed as successful, I found a way to pretend: the clothing that I wore with the tags still attached so I could return them after I had worn them once because I couldn't really afford them; the ambitious front I portrayed when inwardly, and in secret, I had no motivation to work and no desire to live, getting home from work and falling asleep on the couch fully clothed; going to college part-time just to be able to say I was in college; the pigsty I hid well by cramming junk under my bed or in unseen places. It was draining, but it was all part of my great cover-up. No one would love the real me if I didn't even like me. It was an outward manifestation of the internal perspective of my poor self-image; a lack of revelation in knowing whose I am and in whose image I was created.

Jeremiah 17:9-10 MSG
Luke 16:15 GNT
Ephesians 4:22 AMPC

God shows his love for us...
while we were still sinners ...

Romans 5:8 ESV

He had the nerve to text me the day after, "Your development in life often comes by how you react to adverse circumstances you encounter, and how you react is a clear indication of who you are," or some crap like that! I met this guy at a nightclub. I was luring this great dancer over with my sexual tendencies, but I knew that no matter what, I was *not* going to have sex with him. I wasn't into him like that. He was a medical professional in the army and he was only in town for a week – that was perfect enough for me. I was not looking for anything long-term with him. I was attracted to who he said he was, his uniform, and money. This would only serve as something I could put on my dating resume. I was building a portfolio of all the men I was romantically linked with and I wanted it to be impressive.

I thought I was playing my cards very well for all the fine wining and dining, and he clearly was in it for another thing. I found myself in his hotel room two days after meeting him. In the blink of an eye we were on his bed, kissing, then in a matter of seconds, he managed – on his own and in my total surprise – to get fully naked. I knew that there was no way I was touching him. I got extremely nervous, but maintained my composure and somehow managed to calmly get us both off the bed and lead him to the door. He sensed my paranoia and cornered me up against the door. A struggle ensued as I tried to get this naked man off of me. I pushed him off long enough to get the door open, immediately coming face to face with another uniformed man. I was so afraid for my life that I thought perhaps he was conspiring with the naked man inside. All I could do was run. I found the floor where I had parked my vehicle and fumbled for my car-keys. Once inside, I locked my doors as he came rounding the corner. As I sped away, he was screaming something unintelligible, flailing his arms in the air.

I never responded to his text the following day, to this man who I felt would have raped me. To this day I don't remember the man's name, nor would I recognize him if he were before me. I was used to pushing the limits where guys were concerned. I didn't value myself enough to regard my body as precious. I was merely thinking of how I could get what I wanted in life by deceitfully seducing another human being.

Proverbs 7:21 GWT, Ephesians 5:5 AMPC, 1 Corinthians 6:18-20 NLT

*It's
in Christ
that we find out
who we are
and what we are
living for.*

Ephesians 1:11 MSG

Accepting Jesus

I was living my subpar life, struggling to survive emotionally, physically and mentally after having been cheated on by a long-time boyfriend, the night I saw my brother collapse onto the floor like a ton of bricks in a full on seizure. Never had I witnessed such a sight, and never had he experienced such an attack. Throwing all personal etiquette aside, I screamed for help. A woman trained in health care jumped on my brother and slapped him back into consciousness.

I drove him to the ER that evening and under my breath I made a promise: if indeed there was a God and He was listening, I gave Him my word that I would go to church every Sunday for the rest of my life *if* nothing was wrong with my younger brother.

CT scans and neurological tests were performed into the early morning hours. The results: he was perfectly healthy. That was the first and last time he experienced a seizure.

I believe God answered my prayer. So there began my journey of faith. My brother had absolutely no idea about the lifetime commitment I was determined to uphold as I passed his bedroom on my way to church every Sunday morning while he slept-in. He also wouldn't know how, months into my conversion, I had an emotional breakdown. There was a sense of failure that lined my life, and a sense of hopelessness I couldn't shake off. I remember running home to my apartment, straight to my bedroom, and as I dropped to my knees, sobbing, the only thing in view to cling to was a phone book. Clutching it to my chest in desperation, I huddled up in a ball, and when my grip eventually gave way, the book fell to the floor, its pages landing open to the churches section. There it was, the half-page ad of the very church I attended staring out. I called. They put me through to the priest assuming I was suicidal…

The following day I met with Elda Maria who would encourage me in the early stages of my walk, telling me "it takes time". Faith takes time. The things of God take time. And she encouraged me to not give up… that the Word of God would change my life *if* I didn't quit.

Psalm 38:4-9 NLT
Psalm 18:6 NLT
Hebrews 10:36 NLT

These people honor me with their lips,

but their heart

is far from me.

Matthew 15:8 NIV

I was raised Catholic, the kind a preacher once described as a "CEO Christian". You know, those who attend on Christmas and Easter Only. I did what was necessary to receive the sacraments (Baptism, Confirmation, First Communion) of course. I memorized prayers and motions mostly by observation of other congregants during those times.

I was enviously aware of the couples sitting together in Mass; the boy with his arms wrapped tenderly around the girl, lovingly holding her hand during the message, and during the sign of peace, a kiss substituted for the handshake or embrace. This was my focus the entire message.

I had never taken a boy to church. My college roommate, who was more Catholic than me, invited my new boyfriend (who was not Catholic) and me to church with her once. I went, not to seek after God, but so I could cross off one of my "#relationshipgoals". But, there would be no romantic arm around my shoulders, and I was the one who made sure we held hands during the entire service. I awkwardly went to kiss his lips in exchange for peace, void of emotion. Pointless. He later would recount the story with a deep belly laugh describing how I wanted to "get it on" in church. It was an epic fail. I was left with an empty feeling and an embarrassing memory.

The "religion" label did as much for me as the insignificant amount of time I spent at church. It was all in vain. My family believed the only things required to be pleasing to God were in performing the sacraments. To me, they were merely traditions that made the Word of God all to no effect in my life, actions that lacked reverence. Simply a duty to who I believed to be an imaginary God.

Isaiah 29:13 MSG
Mark 7:6-9 GWT
1 Timothy 4:6-10 MSG

*Jesus came
that I might have life,
and have it more abundantly...*

John 10:10 KJV

I came from a background of brokenness, a far cry from what I was supposed to be as a Christian. I was angry, defeated, sad, depressed, in debt, especially fearful where my health was concerned. Surgeries, pain, and constant discomfort were the norm; everything contrary to what I read about in God's Word. I was lost, living amongst others who were just as lost and confused. When I professed Jesus as Lord, it all didn't go away.

Where my health was concerned – fear continually harassed me. I couldn't shut it off. I didn't know how to shut it out. My explosive temper – everything was a trigger that would set my insides raging and blood boiling over with negative emotions. During these trials, the answer was always the same: only believe.

So I began to step out and believe Jesus for healing without medication, and eventually, the pain went away. I have gone eight years now with no medication or surgeries. Slowly, my hostile reactions began to minimize in intensity and were replaced with peace as I spent time with Jesus. I began to amass trophies of my victories in the areas of fear, anger, and sickness. And it is with these rare trophies situated on the shelves of my heart that I could ever consider writing this book.

The most difficult thing in this faith walk has been *"believing";* in God, in Jesus, a Holy Spirit... "Only believe," the word says. The core of my being tells me that I have yet to tap into all that really belongs to me. I know there is more...

> Luke 8:41-55 ESV
> John 6:28-29 NIV
> Mark 9:23-24 AMP

...*You have made me into a helpmeet for him.*

Genesis 2:18 KJV

My focus was once that he (my husband) shouldn't be alone, that he was not created to be without me. I have come to realize that God is a God of purpose and intention. I have a part to play in all this as well. I have discovered that God was and is molding me by repairing me, shaping me, and preparing me…

My emotions were always plagued with a gnawing feeling —something is missing; something is broken. And indeed there was, but not in the sense of me being alone or not having someone. It was my *character* that was lacking, my *thinking* distorted and defeated.

My self-esteem was shot. The tune in my head was a broken record of inadequacies. I didn't know my purpose. I just wanted someone to hold me and give me validation as a human. My self worth was measured by finding someone to love me. My skewed thinking had me persuaded that it didn't matter if I actually loved *them* – it was all about what I needed them to do for *me*. My insides were battered, bruised, bleeding, and seething. I had such a disdain of self that those who knew me best would taste that wrath and anger time and time again. My whole life consisted of me. I was *consumed* with *me*.

But as I have read, studied, meditated, and hungered after the things of God, He began putting me back together. God's peace reverberated into the dark tumultuous pit of my soul, igniting a purpose beyond marriage, reviving a life which aspires to honor and glorify Him as an individual first, one capable of being used by Him to fulfill a perfect plan that *includes* being of help to another.

James 4:1-3 AMPC
Philippians 2:3-5 NASB
Jeremiah 17:14 MSG

...and having done all to stand,

STAND...

Ephesians 6:13-14 KJV

It wasn't until very recently that I actually voiced aloud to others this immense desire to be married. My resolve was to stay strong, poker face intact, dodging questions and concealing my left hand out of shame for being single. I never led on that I ever cared for a married life except to a very limited few.

Earlier in the year we were wrapping up a book study about dreams and goals using vision boards. Everyone was asked to share, so with goal book in hand, I let down all my defenses, and passed my book around that contained the very life words, images and scriptures that were carrying me through this single season.

That moment was very liberating, yet it left me wide open to questions and comments. But it didn't shame me like I thought it would. If anything, having to field questions from others solidified to me how truly deep my desire is to walk in the things of God, to follow God blamelessly, to live a life demonstrating and proving God's very existence and goodness for people to see.

I want to be part of a generation that no longer compromises. A generation that is willing to hold out. A generation that is willing to stand our ground, and when we have done all to stand, we continue standing on the promises of God for our lives. Not giving into the pressure of forcing things to happen in our own might, but living life seeing God make things happen for us, with us, and through us. No pretense. No lies. No covering up. No regrets, just blameless before God and man.

Psalm 24:4-6 NET
Hebrews 10:35-36 NLT
Exodus 34:10 NIV

*Am I now
seeking the approval of man,
or of God?*

Galatians 1:10 ESV

"Today was easier than yesterday, than the past four days... I was hoping to hear back from this guy. What did I do wrong? Ugh! I busied myself today – It wasn't until I got in the car to drive home did I start feeling that loneliness... longing... I just want to be in love. Why didn't he like me, Lord?" – Journal entry, 2013

I never brought boys home for Thanksgiving – ever. Having become recently more vocal about desiring a relationship, my cousin was quick to tell me about a handsome guy who was new in town. She immediately got on her phone and invited him over for our family Thanksgiving dinner as my blind date.

He came. No sparks, only awkwardness from the moment he arrived; having just been introduced outside that cold, wet night, and the fact that all my family was watching every move between us.

At the end of the night, he asked my cousin for my phone number. I unenthusiastically gave her the ok – willfully overlooking all the awkwardness, even his age (he was younger than me). I had been waiting a long time to fall in love – anyone would do.

It took him two days before he texted me. Not once did he pick up his phone to actually speak to me. I secretly spent my days wishing and hoping he would. Days, and sometimes weeks, would go by before I would get another text from him. But I was at his beck and call... Such as the night he texted close to midnight – I was already in bed. With work the following day, I was a little perturbed as to why he would text me so late... he was out with friends drinking.

I chose to overlook all the signs. He didn't ask *me* for my phone number; he never *called* me, not once; he never asked me *about* me. Desperate, I was willing to jump head first into this relationship, if he would have only been interested in me the slightest bit.

I didn't want to be alone anymore. I knowingly and willingly chose denial because I just wanted to be in love. I didn't even like the guy, but I still wanted him to like me and pursue me.

Psalm 25:16 AMP
Proverbs 16:1-2 NLT
Proverbs 14:12-13 MSG

...you are only fooling yourself.

Galatians 6:3 NLT

He cheated on me. On Valentine's Day he got me nothing. Maybe because it was *her* he spent his money on. When he came asking for forgiveness, he brought a week late Valentine's gift of cheap, ill-looking flowers. Infuriated, I trashed them in the dumpster. After minimal persistence by him, I gave in and agreed to stay with him. Blinded by jealousy and driven by hurt, my heart, now, more than ever, was not in it. Yet, I stayed because I believed that no one would ever love me like he did, treat me like he did, or at least that is what he would say to me, and that is what I believed. The thought of finding another guy who would be interested in me seemed too difficult.

I kept going back to him because our souls, over the span of two years, had become entangled, through our physical contact having gone too far, and as we confided in each other about our deepest secrets, fears, and dreams. Although I distrusted him now, I willingly chose to overlook his cheating for the sake of not being alone. The busyness of our frequent dates and never-ending drama temporarily filled the emptiness I felt. The loneliness I feared was covered by hugs and kisses. My heavy insecurities were lightened by his presence.

The betrayal should have been a *further* indication that something was missing, something was lacking in this relationship, in our characters, and in our lives. We were both in a relationship we were never intended to cultivate to the depths at which we did. The familiarity with which we interacted should have been reserved for my husband. And clearly, he was not my husband.

James 3:16 AMP
Romans 6:12-14 AMP
Titus 3:3-6 NIV

I put away childish things.

1 Corinthians 13:11 NLT

I had missed out on the dating scene for most of my high school years so I was making up for lost time. I was in college now and the list of boys I made out with kept increasing; a list I secretly kept in my personal notebook. I never committed to those boys because I sensed that there was always someone better, so I kept going through the numbers in hopes that one day I would come across "the one".

Oh, how I enjoyed playing the game – teasing these boys. The names I couldn't remember, I listed anyway, by note of something I remembered about them – their height or the color of their shirt. How powerful I felt when I had them eating out of the palm of my hand, pretending they might get lucky with me that night, knowing full well that I would never deliver. I was searching for the one I could totally trust, commit, love, give my life to… mind, soul and body without reservations, hesitations or hidden agendas. I couldn't commit when my heart was feeling as though something was missing, something I just couldn't put my finger on.

The one my heart longed for, the one my heart craved, the one my heart yearned for was unequivocally Jesus. No amount of men or dates was ever going to be enough to satisfy such a deep deficiency. All along, Jesus was patiently waiting, knowing full well that one day I would turn to Him, that one day I would realize that it was He my heart hungered for. My heart was already spoken for long before I was born.

Song of Solomon 8:7 TLB
Ecclesiastes 3:11 AMP
Deuteronomy 4:29 AMPC

...God has been with you...

Deuteronomy 2:7 NIV

I met him towards the end of my first year in college. He was one of the cutest boys I had ever met AND he was interested in me! He was so dreamy, so fine! Those were the only qualities I was looking for in a boyfriend. I had never experienced such sensations in my body as I did when his full lips first kissed mine. All my senses were heightened to a new awareness, my heart pounding in new places. I became intoxicated and my judgment was clouded with his touch, his taste, his smell, our contact, as he skillfully pressed our bodies close and tight.

When I went home for the summer we kept in touch over the phone. I can vividly remember one conversation where he was laughing so hard he could barely speak. He was with a group of friends trying to best describe their scenario...something about a dancing monkey. I think he was high.

When I got back to college in the fall, I didn't want him to get in touch with me. I had a strong sense, that if I continued seeing him, he would take a thing that was important to me – my virginity, leaving me heartbroken. My gut was warning me against this boy. So I didn't inform him when I'd be back in town, and I never gave him my new phone number and address. I did second-guess myself, wondering what became of him, if he ever attempted to call me, or made any effort to find me.

Years later, I randomly ran into him. He had changed, I had changed, and what was once there, no longer was. It was *so hard* making the decision to walk away at the time, but I knew I had to do it. I was so far removed from God that He couldn't have been my reason for rejecting this opportunity of being held, kissed, loved, wanted and desired.

A still small voice was guiding me, even then. A voice of reason was there, in the very center of my gut. I now recognize it as God's protection over my life even when I wasn't following or pursuing Him. Many times I put myself in compromising positions, fully aware of what I was doing, and that unsettled feeling in the pit of my stomach would randomly appear, warning me about committing acts I would ultimately regret.

Isaiah 30:21 NIV
Matthew 28:20 AMP
Jonah 1:1-3 MSG

My help comes from the Lord...

Psalm 121:2 NIV

"Cómo estás?"
"Hola, aquí platicando con Dios."
"Que bonito."

"How are you?"
"Hi. Here talking to God."
"How beautiful."

In actuality, I wanted to tell this person over the phone that I was weeping. I was hurting because of a broken friend-relationship. In fact, I was praying to God to bring comfort to my soul.

My dependence once rested on human beings, desperately seeking their advice for my life's situations, unloading my emotional baggage so they could point me in the right direction. My confidence was based on their approval of my choices. I sought out people who appeared to have it all together so that they could reason out my life and guide me to figure it out. Many times I followed their advice, good or bad. I just wanted and needed help.

Even in my faith walk, I have reasoned with God in moments like these, that I need my mate *N O W*, to talk to, to hug, and affirm me as a human being. "That's why *I'M* here," God whispers… It's not the first time God has reminded me where my dependence should lay, and where my help should come from.

God created me, and only He, with the help of the Holy Spirit, will be able to guide me through the treacherous waters of life's relationships. I am thankful for the individuals who I once placed my reliance on, but my true comfort and solid answers can only come from God:

Reassurance when I doubted in the existence of God;
Guidance as I questioned to understand my purpose;
Relief when I was tormented and despised myself;
Compassion in the midst of anger when I feel wronged by others;
Fortitude during the times I feel most alone.

Psalm 46:1 AMP
John 14:17-18 AMPC
John 14:26-27 AMP

*Now to Him who is able
to carry out His purpose
and do superabundantly more
than all that we dare ask or think,
infinitely beyond our greatest prayers,
hopes, or dreams...*

Ephesians 3:20 AMP

My Dream Man

I first heard about declaring and speaking forth my future when I joined a direct sales business team. We were encouraged to create dream boards for goals that included images of material things we hoped to one day possess. The yet-to-be-married were even encouraged to make a list of qualities we desired of our future mate. In one sitting, I had a hundred reasonable and unreasonable qualities – I mean, why can't I ask for a 6'2", left-handed, blue-eyed, non-tatted, hairless-chested, Latino!

One day as I was admiring the list about my dream man, contemplating even more qualities, my daydreaming came to a screeching halt. I sensed God telling me to throw the list away. This could not have been my own idea. I would never, ever, propose such a reckless act on the paper I had beautifully and intentionally hand-crafted to illustrate my future. I also sensed Him saying that I was limiting Him (God). Desperately wanting to hold on to my dream man, I wrestled with God to keep him, but I heard nothing more from God on the topic. I had a confidence telling me that this is what faith is about – trusting that the words spoken to my heart were from God; hope, my only evidence. So amidst complete inner turmoil, I grabbed the paper, ripped it into pieces, and hurriedly ran to the dumpster outside. Had I wasted anymore time, or thrown it away within reach, I would have dug it out of the trash and pieced it back together.

What I realize today is that God gives us clues: longings and desires. Not so I can try to force something to happen out of my own efforts, but as the encouragement needed to trust His plans for me, especially during the wilderness seasons of loneliness. He speaks to me through His Word, renewing my mind, refreshing my soul, encouraging me to not lose hope, to keep my eyes focused on Him, because as I continually seek Him first, He will ultimately lead me to desires far more than what I could have ever imagined, dreamed of, or conceived on my own.

On several occasions since, God has spoken to my heart specifically about this man, my husband, and the qualities and traits he will possess. I will recognize him at the right and opportune time. These qualities spoken to me by God about my husband are now written on the tablets of my heart.

Proverbs 16:1-3 NLT
Proverbs 19:20-21 NIV
Habakkuk 2:2-3 MSG

Speak the word only.

Matthew 8:8 KJV

I remember my pastor saying that if we want to pray for someone, we should pray scripturally. He challenged each one sitting in the meeting that day to pray the Ephesians prayer if our desire was to have an effective prayer life for others. So I did, for each one of my eight family members, not really certain what the end result of these prayers would be. I truly believed if my family gave their lives to this Jesus I now loved, their lives would be radically transformed. Several months in, I encouraged my sister to pray with me. Within three months of our agreeing prayers, voicing them out loud daily, every last one of our immediate family members accepted Jesus as their Lord.

A few years later, I encountered some challenging times where my health was concerned and got a hold of a book by Charles Capps. I took the verses he lined out from the Bible like medicine, speaking them over myself in the morning, in the afternoon and in the evening. Three years later, I received complete healing in my body. Multiple times God has reminded me that the way I obtained the promises of eternal salvation and healing would be the same way of receiving for every area of my life.

Over the course of the last seven years, what I have spoken over my life has changed. I didn't believe that I could or would ever be married, and that perhaps marriage was not in my destiny. But the desire was so deeply seeded I couldn't shake it off. So, the first place of business was the scripture that says it is not good that man should be alone, and that God made me a helpmeet for a man. I began speaking that over myself. Not vain, empty, thoughtless words, but purposeful words, spoken so that I could shut out the noise telling me that it would never happen in my life.

I have seen this principle of speaking the Word of God work in my life. I do it to renew my mind, to replace old ways of thinking, to believe that what God has promised will happen. I do it because I have got to believe what the Bible says when it speaks of *the Word* of God being *seed*; seed that will produce if I keep on watering it as I open my mouth and continually declare what is written.

Ephesians 1:16-18 NIV
Luke 8:11 KJV
Mark 5:28 BSB

*...and this is only the beginning
of what they will do,*

*and now nothing they have imagined
they can do will be impossible
for them...*

Genesis 11:6 AMPC

Coincidence? I Think Not

I was flipping through the TV when a young man on a local channel caught my eye and captivated my attention. I had never seen him nor did I know who he was, but the words that I spoke out of my mouth in that instance were, "I am going to marry that man." A few years came and went, and through a series of multiple events I purposely positioned myself to try to meet him and we eventually ran into each other. We scheduled a lunch date, but just hours before we were to sit opposite each other, he cancelled. Something in his job had come up.

I was once of the opinion that one's convictions and actions could be overlooked by the size of one's bank account. That man went on to marry someone else. I have seen him in the media a few times since then and I cringe each time I hear his name, especially with the political associations and social platforms he esteems and supports. My life would have been a complete disaster.

The Word I had been feeding my soul over the course of that time had been changing my mindset from when I first spoke such reckless thoughts aloud. I was driving the moment I realized he was not who I wanted. It was like a veil had been ripped from my eyes. In my car I screamed, cancelling those foolish words I had spoken over my life years earlier in regards to this man. I recognized that it wasn't by chance that we met; it was something I had created. I realized that from the moment I spoke and repeated those careless words, I had set off a biblical principle.

At times I have rolled my eyes at the absurdity that simply declaring words out loud would have any power in themselves. But I have no other explanation for the transforming results I have experienced from when I began to guard my tongue and the words I allowed out of my mouth. Changes happened as my words changed.

Proverbs 18:21 ISV
Proverbs 13:3 NIV
Proverbs 21:23 NLT

I do believe;
help me overcome my unbelief!

Mark 9:24 NIV

I was no stranger to sickness, chronic pain, medication, or doctors. As a child I seemed to always suffer from some ailment. In my teens I discovered a lump in my breast. I was plagued with random bouts of severe pain, repeatedly misdiagnosed, and had two cancer-scare surgeries by the time I reached my early twenties.

One evening in the spring of 2008, a pain shot into my shoulder and down my right arm. I consulted the doctor the following day and got a steroid shot. As the week progressed the pain intensified, spreading itself into my entire upper right torso. I went back for further testing. The results were inconclusive. Popping prescription pain medication ensued morning, noon, and night to prevent them wearing off, that is until the evening they finally took a toll on my body. My heart began to race uncontrollably; the stress of processing a foreign substance day in and day out was too great for my emaciated body.

That night I told God I was *not* going to take the medication anymore. Instead, I would trust Him for *t h e* healing the Bible speaks about, the same healing I had heard preached for three years: Jesus came to heal *me*, and by His stripes *I am* healed. I took God's Word at face value. The dread of cancer, or worse yet, death, loomed over me. I was afraid. I was alone. But I didn't allow myself to speak of the pain and fear, not to myself or anyone else. I would lay prostrate, face to the floor, in the days, months, and years that followed, uttering healing scriptures, reminding myself and God about His Word, all the while, doubting in my head and heart. The pain was real.

I could no longer idly say whatever words I wanted to say. I had to get to the point where I believed that the words I said in the name of Jesus had power to change my mindset and present circumstances. And over the course of those three years the pain would subside momentarily then return, but each time it took longer to come back. Although disappointment tried to set it each time it returned, I continued confessing the word of God, as I had nowhere else to turn, and eventually the pain, along with any traces of it, disappeared completely. Victory.

Matthew 4:4 AMP
Hebrews 10:23 AMPC
Deuteronomy 32:47 NIV

Your desire and longing will be for your husband...

Genesis 3:16 AMP

"Lord, I was so excited by what YOU spoke to my heart today! You told me that my future spouse would pursue me and that he would win my heart. It was just comforting because lately I've felt as though I am the one who has always done the pursuing..." – Journal Entry, 2005

...such as the guy that I stalked (yeah, that's right!) who was a frequent customer at the shipping service center where I worked at the time. I made sure to get in front of his eyes. I even copied down his address and phone number so I could scope out his neighborhood before calling him. Then there was the politician. He was super easy to track. I made believe we had the same interests when we showed up at the same places...what a coincidence! He had a girlfriend, but that didn't stop me.

I was used to seeing women taking the initiative and manipulating the course of relationships. It seemed like the girls who were brazen enough to make the first move were the ones having all the fun, so by taking matters into my own hands, by copy of what I had observed, life became exciting – I was going on dates! Men didn't have a chance to pursue me for fear of another woman beating me to the punch, especially if he was an eligible bachelor. They didn't stay single too long in a world of free-agent single females. It was a devouring longing that made me think irrationally. I was pursuing men to control a needy desire of being wanted and pursued myself. Nothing was off limits, stalking, provocative words and actions, teasing, flirting...

This longing was what the fall of man had produced. When the blessing lifted, womankind was left desiring a husband, a human, in place of God. The pursuing got distorted. Such a longing to belong to another human is actually contrary to the very nature of our creation. That longing, that yearning in the core of my being to be loved and desired is only utterly fulfilled by the One who knows how to cherish and fulfill me best – my Creator. God had a redemptive plan to win me back by coming as a man, spreading His arms on a cross, shedding His blood even until death. Rising from death He *still* comes for me. What greater form of pursuit can there be?

Song of Solomon 5:2-8 NIV
Proverbs 7:10-18 MSG
Isaiah 4:1 NIV

But don't just listen to God's word.

You must do what it says.

Otherwise,

you are only fooling yourselves.

James 1:22 NLT

I met him while attending the mega church we both frequented. I had eyed him for weeks before he finally approached me! I remember getting into my car as seductively as I could, knowing he was standing behind me. I gave him my number as immediately as he asked for it. He was a sharp looking, very well dressed, pharmaceutical rep with a nice smile, who also carried himself exceptionally well and lived in a ritzy downtown condo. We spent most of our time talking on the phone. When he finally asked me to lunch, I recall that I paid for my own meal. A couple of days later, he invited me over to his place so we could get into his Jacuzzi. Desperate for a relationship, and in spite of all my apprehension, I agreed. The plan was for me to call him while on my way so he could give me his address, but when I called he didn't answer. I dialed his number a few more times… still no answer. I pulled into a restaurant parking lot to await a call back. Disappointed, I headed home long after the world was asleep.

A few days later, he called to explain why we couldn't continue talking. Somehow, he said, he knew I wouldn't sleep with him. And for him, that was extremely important. How else would he know if I was the one, he reasoned: plain and simple. I was astonished at his words. A *Christian*. I don't know if he wanted me to dispel his belief, but there was no pleading my case. I simply said, "You're right." And that was the end of that.

Simply going to church and going through motions does not make a Christian. Calling ourselves Christians, while embracing sin, stops the power and authority God wants to demonstrate through our lives. While I was not willing to have sex with him, I was ready to tease him, stopping only short of it, making my actions equally inexcusable. We both wanted something from each other. He was forthright with his expectations of the relationship. I was deviously willing to compromise my body, in return for nice dinners and a boy to call my own.

2 Timothy 3:2-7 NIV
2 Timothy 3:2-7 AMP
James 1:22-25 AMP

Teach me,

                and I will hold my tongue:
and cause me to understand

where I have erred.

Job 6:24 KJV

"You're lazy, boring, annoying, stingy, a hypocrite, selfish, undisciplined, and a free-loader. Be realistic!" he said. But for some reason I kept going back.
— Journal Entry, 2007

In two of my longest standing relationships, both guys said that women like me were "a dime a dozen". In the same breath, one of them went on to tell me how my low self-esteem was a turn-off. I was not unaccustomed to being called ugly names or *being* the person who said hurtful things to others. Though I am certain these words were spoken to me and by me in a moment of rage, hurtful words are still hurtful. Some journal entries are a harsh reminder of the person I once was.

One day in a counseling session with my pastor, with unreserved trust and extreme vulnerability, I shared about the negative, cursing words that were spoken over me repeatedly during my childhood, ashamedly voicing them out loud, weeping with such deep bitterness, unaware of the buried hurt I had held onto for all those years. The negative words I, in turn, spoke over others were a direct reflection of what my heart was full of: hurt, anger, resentment. Each time a negative thing was said to me, I hardened my heart to that person, vowing that they would never hurt me again as I unleashed equally destructive words over their lives in retaliation.

I would like to think that the girl who penned these journal entries no longer sees herself, or behaves, in the manner those negative words describe, and that outdated history book has been replaced by another book. The words on the pages of the Bible speak of the person I was created to be; words that speak of me being fearfully and wonderfully made; the head and not the tail; words that encourage me to lift my head and arise from the great depression in which past circumstances had kept me; that I have been completely forgiven and set free, that I am precious in His eyes, honored, and so loved.

It's *His* story for my life I now choose to speak and believe over myself, and over others.

Matthew 12:34-36 AMPC
James 3:3-12 MSG
Ephesians 4:29 AMP

Let your 'Yes' be 'Yes,' and your 'No,' 'NO.'

Matthew 5:37 BSB

"The guy from work that I'm so attracted to invited me to the lake this weekend. I told him no automatically. He told me to think about it. There was nothing to think about... It was awkward just standing there, both of us mute. He then shrugged it off like it was no big deal. I wanted him to persist, to pursue me in a real way, but he didn't." – Journal Entry, 2007

    I only rejected his advances because I wanted to keep my word to God. Around this time on my journey, I had become keenly aware of my difficulty saying "NO" to anyone. I felt obligated to do things because I didn't have the self-esteem to refuse anyone anything. A few weeks before this encounter I made a commitment to say "I'm busy" if anybody, especially men, requested my time, because I wanted to invest my time studying God's Word. I struggled with that decision when the opportunity I had secretly desired (for years!) was right before me slipping away.

    I was in a season of desperation – I wanted my life to change, to have meaning! And I didn't know how to "make" God's Word work, or how to tap into His promises of peace, hope, and a brighter future. I had no guide, no quick-start instruction manual. I simply had a will for my life to change from meaningless, empty, worthless, and hollow to something significant. Everything else I had tried failed me, or I had failed it, but something was different with God's Word. Life's challenges didn't cease right away. On the contrary, some intensified. So with Bible in hand, I read more, I studied more, I spoke more, I raised my hands to heaven more, and each time I prayed or meditated I felt an increasing calmness. I had a peace I had never experienced before.

    That day I stopped short of throwing myself onto this man and wrapping my legs around his waist, as I had often envisioned myself doing. Unbeknownst to me, the word I had been sowing into the soil of my heart was taking root, creating boundaries where there was once no restraint.

Galatians 1:10 ESV
2 Timothy 1:7 AMPC
Philippians 4:7 NLT

above...
is from
Gift
Perfect
and
Good
Every

James 1:17 NIV

I think it is human nature to believe that I know what's best for me. It can be so difficult to believe in a God who seems so far away and who appears to remain mute most of the time, to know what is best for me. How can I trust what appears to be an absentee Father when I'm struggling through challenges alone? It was *my own* efforts that got me out of that small town. *I* stepped out to pursue the next "better" job. *I* get up day after day to make a living. The burden of making things happen has always fallen on me, especially in relationships, so why should I not trust that I can also make important decisions where men and marriage are concerned on my own?

Sure, I was in complete control with my $13K car note that I struggled to pay each month, with the many letters and calls from the bank wanting their money or their car. I jumped from job to job due to lack of purpose. I lived in a tiny apartment with no table, no TV, and only one seating place. I cycled though physical pain, sickness, medical doctors, surgeries and medicines for unknown diagnoses. Oh, and I can't forget the many broken relationships that filled my life.

It took small nudges from God – such as being a good steward with my employer as I began to serve them honestly with my time and their supplies. I got passionate about healing – looking up the scriptures from Genesis to Revelation. And as for my relationships, I allowed God to show me my distorted code of conduct with men, and ultimately made a conscious choice to change my *modus operandi*. I no longer found it appropriate to tease or rub up against men to get my way.

I was not ready to receive such blessings with a broken integrity, or receive my healing when my faith was in men and medication. With God, I have been given a car debt-free. This sleeping giant of entrepreneurship awoke. I am an author! I have gone eight years without medications or surgeries. I live in a home full of antique furnishings I didn't have to invest one penny in. I have clarity where there was once confusion about my life and purpose.

1 Corinthians 8:2 NIV
Matthew 7:11 NLT
Psalm 84:11 ESV

...Forget the former things.

Isaiah 43:18 NIV

"My God, My God, My God! How could I not love YOU? How could I not trust YOU when time after time you have proven YOURSELF faithful and have never failed me? Even today as my soul is at great peace regarding this man, YOU indeed are good to me; even as my emotions get tangled in this web we call life, when profanity still vandalizes my thoughts and lustful images still haunt me from a life I lived long ago. Yet, YOU remain the same, my constant, my peace, my everything." – Journal Entry, 2016

We all have a past. Some have visible scars. Others, well, not so visible or even apparent, but we know exactly where they are and how they got there. It's our own story. Understanding our own story and the ability to separate who we are from that past lies in understanding the difference between soul and spirit. They used to mean the same thing to me, but they are very different. My soul is my mind, my will, and my emotions. At the core of it, it is my very *human* nature. My soul was ruler of it all, and it contains remnants of the person I used to be. My *spirit* is the essence of who God created me to be, who I really am, and its communion with God is paramount to walking out the rest of my story, the way God originally wrote it.

I already mentioned a few challenges I faced in relationships, but the gist of that story is that I was looking for someone to fill a void; a longing to be accepted and loved. Truth be told, I wasn't even fully committed to any of those relationships. I kept my options open, always. I wasn't in love, but I had allowed my soul to become emotionally tangled in a web of deceit. I had placed my trust in men, basing their integrity solely on good looks, not realizing that other hurt and broken souls would ultimately hurt and break me, falling into traps I would later lament:

the regret of physically giving more of myself than I should have;
the sting of being cheated on;
the humiliation of being talked down to in public and in front of friends;
and the narrow escape from being raped.

Isaiah 43:18-19 CEB
Romans 6:4 AMPC
2 Corinthians 5:17 NLT

*Plans fail without advice,
but with many counselors
they are confirmed.*

Proverbs 15:22 ISV

I had been on this faith journey a short time when we crossed paths, but I knew beyond a shadow of a doubt that he was not the one for me. I played the game anyway. I deeply craved to be a part of a relationship – anything was better than nothing. Someone was better than no one, and because *I* already knew he was not my knight in shining armor, *I* would hold the upper hand, as usual.

A friend had once encouraged me to get my vertical alignment with God right, first, before I tried to do anything horizontally, so during this time I also began to seek spiritual council within the new church I was attending. I knew I needed help with this newly found life of faith. While my unsettled spirit prompted me to seek guidance about this relationship, my head was trying to convince me to keep it secret.

Ultimately, I did address the situation; the day "Mr. Right Now" drove me to one of my counseling appointments and sat outside in his truck. Inside, the firm, authoritative voice behind the desk said, "You are not ready for a relationship." It only confirmed what I already knew. My mind then set to racing about how to devise a game plan to backtrack out of the knee high mess I was already in, and how I would make it out of this meeting without anyone knowing who I had waiting just outside!

I still counsel with my pastors regarding many areas of my life, but the counseling was not effective until I could be honest with them and honest with myself, totally letting all my guards down, believing they have my best interests in mind. I had a track record of broken relationships, and in each one, I was the common denominator. My pastors have unconditionally held my hand along this path until I trusted myself enough to walk on my own.

Proverbs 11:14 KJV
Hebrews 13:17 AMP
Ruth 3 AMPC

What shall we say then?

Shall we continue in sin, that grace may abound?

Romans 6:1 KJV

Just as I Am

We found ourselves in his apartment again, fully clothed, but still, rolling around in the dark. When he hit the lights back on, right in the center of the bed lay my cross, in plain view. Embarrassed, I quickly snatched it but not before seeing the look of alarm on his face; his eyes wide open as if he had seen a ghost; neither one of us made mention of that moment, ever.

While I was beginning to hunger for more of God's presence in my life, I began carrying a small cross in my pocket. I began talking to Him more frequently and was going to the chapel daily. The heaviness I had carried around for years was beginning to dissipate. Just touching that cross gave me comfort no matter where I was. I clung to that token like it was my lifeline. I also did it as a cue to remember Him; I wanted to be more aware of God in my daily life. When I got busy it seemed like the last thing on my mind was God. The cross was a simple reminder for me to think about Him.

But my life was still very much full of compromise. I still behaved inappropriately with boys, keeping some relationships secret as well as my behavior with guys behind closed doors. The crazy thing was that I wasn't bothered by any of this conduct. Surely if my behavior was wrong, I would have sensed some form of condemnation from God, right?

As I was continuing to develop my faith, becoming more highly aware of God's protective presence, my thoughts and actions were bringing their own convictions. Each time I "messed up" I would ask God for His forgiveness, and each time I sensed a comforting peace. Ultimately, I stopped romping with boys, not because of condemnation from God, but because of how much God continually demonstrated His love towards me. I could sense it. I could feel it, and I knew it. UNCONDITONAL LOVE. He didn't require me to wait until I cleaned up my act or became perfect to come before Him. The more He loved me, the more I desired to please Him where my actions with boys were concerned.

Romans 5:8 AMP
2 Peter 3:8-9 AMPC
Romans 6 MSG

...a still small voice.

1 Kings 19:12 KJV

Fine-Tuning

God was speaking. It was no longer just a gut feeling. God had been speaking to me all along.

It would be one of the last times I would go dancing. I usually danced with many men in a given night; my way of inviting as many men as possible to approach me in hopes of finding the one. This night I broke protocol and danced the night away with just one. He said he felt I was heaven-sent, as if our meeting were by divine appointment. And he seemed perfect to me; tall, attractive, Latino… but I couldn't bring myself to give him my number. His pleas and reasoning were not enough. I discreetly slipped away early that night so he wouldn't come after me, cautiously looking over my shoulder. I had a strange feeling about him, as if he were hiding something. He wore no wedding band, but he *seemed* married.

At different times – and in very odd circumstances like this one – I didn't have a clear understanding about why I just knew certain things. But what I did have now, was *the Word*. I was putting the Word of God in my mind, in my heart, and voicing it out of my mouth. As the young man spoke to me, I had absolutely no substantial evidence that called for me to reject his advances, but the unrest in my gut, the uneasiness that I sensed, the little voice in my head was telling me that *something* was "off"… I believe that it was the Word of God I had been feeding my soul – confessed each day as I awoke, consumed at lunchtime – and the raising up of my arms to heaven before bed that was discerning something "off" about this man.

As I look back on all the "missed opportunities", I don't regret them, *now*. In the moment I did truly regret some of them, and even mourned some of my decisions in the lonely days that followed. I often had gut-feelings, but during this season of my life I began – believing – becoming more aware that the voice of reason in my gut was *God speaking* to me. It was the Holy Spirit, through *the Word of God*, doing His work, even in my early stages of trusting in Him. The Word I was feeding upon was discerning not only my thoughts and intentions, but, also, men's thoughts and intentions.

Isaiah 11:2-3 AMPC
Daniel 2:22 AMP
Hebrews 4:12 AMPC

But if you do not do what is right, sin is crouching at your door; it desires to have you, but you must master it.

Genesis 4:7 NIV

Rejection…Again…

I was now 4 years into my walk when I made the phone call. Just a few months earlier, he pleaded with me to become his girlfriend. Time and time again he insisted, and time and time again I denied him. I was not into him like I was into his profession, his body, and his money. But I let my flesh have its way anyway. And what began as an innocent game turned into an intoxicating and destructive relationship, without the label. In less than 6 months I was blatantly asking him for money – like he owed it to me. And he no longer treated me with respect – calling me names and belittling me in front of his friends, talking down to me, and shutting me up without regard for who was around. We made the decision to stop talking on several occasions, but found ourselves back in each other's arms, repeatedly, until the evening I called him while he was in the company of another female.

In the months leading up to this moment, I kept despising myself for giving into my flesh. Multiple journal entries capture the internal struggle I was facing morally. That call was the last straw I needed to begin framing a life that would be pleasing to God. I was finished doing it my way – living a double life. In my heart I loved Jesus with everything I had, but I was also extremely good at concealing the one area of life that kept me bound in sin. I didn't want the world to find out that my good girl image was a false one, because their condemnation was more fiery than that of a God that only demonstrated love towards me.

The momentary pleasure that my flesh feasted on always left me disappointed. In the moment I was blinded and overcome with a burning passion that seemed like it would rip my body in half if I didn't give in to it, bubbling up in the pit of my stomach, blinding my senses and clouding my sound judgment. In the heat of the moment nothing, or anyone else, mattered. Satisfying my flesh was what my entire mind, will, and emotions were fixated on. The aftermath was only shame, regret, and fear. Subconsciously I knew that call was the final straw. My flesh was losing ground. It's ability to dictate my life according to its pleasure and its will was being extinguished.

Galatians 5:17 NLT
Romans 7:15-25 AMP
Romans 8:1-13 AMP

Your life will be clean,

and you will be ready for the Master to use you

for every good work.

2 Timothy 2:21 NLT

"Why do I feel like this? I hate the very person I am. I've been in such a bad mood. Why? What is wrong with me? Everything bothers me. Why am I like this? Why is my soul missing joy? How can I change? What must I change?"
– Journal Entry, 2008

I remember feeling annoyed with myself and everyone else who was around. I remember being discontent to the very depths of my soul. I was impatient, moody, selfish, needy, greedy, and insecure – definitely not qualities most people desire in their mate. I was not ready for a relationship with a man. But I somehow believed that a boy would fix all the negativity in my life. And indeed it did, for the first few months or so, but then I would slip back into my patterns. The real me would inevitably show up after the excitement and newness of the relationship wore off.

When I began sincerely pursuing God, negative attitudes seemed to manifest to a higher degree. The process felt like a pot of boiling water had been poured down over my soul, exposing attitudes I tried so hard to suppress. I felt miserable as each of these perpetrators surfaced, revealing the broken person I truly was. And as they surfaced, I had to deal with them, acknowledge them, and then choose to remain the same or change. In so many of those instances when I was dealing with an issue, a circumstance would arise that would tug at that old person. I failed time and time and time again in those instances, reverting to the ugly and mean person I so despised.

I was not ready for a relationship with a man. I needed time with God so that He could put me back together instead of me bringing down another human being in my misery. I needed this time with God so He could prepare me for my life's purpose. I was created to be a helper to my husband. Not a hindrance. I needed this time even though it has felt too long and drawn out, and at many times painful. I needed to know God first cares about me individually, before I am to be part of a marriage.

Psalm 51:10 ISV
Colossians 3:8 AMPC
2 Timothy 2:21-24 AMP

*I laid a foundation
as a wise master builder,
and someone else is building on it.*

1 Corinthians 3:10 NIV

My mother was in labor, so all my siblings and I stayed over at a neighbor's house. In their son's room, we were all awestruck with the images coming through on the television screen. Static and grainy, the boys tried their best to fix the rabbit ears so we could see the movie more clearly. It was porn, and we all stood around that screen fascinated by the actions being performed between the man and the woman.

Unbeknownst to everyone, including me, my life was being shaped and molded, foundations being framed by the very things I saw, heard, touched and tasted. I heard about the breast cancer in my maternal grandmother, and the sudden blindness my paternal grandmother experienced. I heard how stupid or incompetent I was from people in authority over my life. I felt the lumps in my breast and the pain in my chest.

That is how I lived for the first twenty-four years of my life. Day in and day out, inundated with negativity, fear, and confusion. I now understand why Elda Maria said, "It takes time…faith takes time. The things of God take time." I have had to replace twenty-four year old mindsets and establish new beliefs, banish fears and control my thoughts, all while learning to rein in my tongue. I am driving out the world and its belief systems, replacing them with the unseen, with the unheard, with the untouched, with the unfelt: Faith. It's a hard concept to understand when we live in a world where everything is based on the five senses.

I once thought that giving my life to Christ would resolve my issues immediately…it didn't. BUT IT DID, over time. No wonder it seems as though this process has taken way too long. I needed time to demolish the life I had framed without Christ and erect a new life, a better life, whose foundation is Christ.

Acts 4:11 NIV
Isaiah 28:16 AMPC
Jeremiah 1:9-10 AMP

*Those who are planted
in the house of the LORD,*

    *they will flourish
in the courts of our God.*

Psalm 92:13 NIV

"I put in my notice of resignation yesterday, and I will admit, I started to doubt... My coworkers asked me if I had a job, a place to live, you know, the "natural" and "obvious" things you need to know before you move, they said. My supervisor said he was worried... another girl laughed, and another asked if I was moving for a boyfriend. One said that would be where I would find the love of my life." – Journal Entry, 2009

Church life was no longer inspiring. I felt like I was only going to check off a box to fulfill my promise, yet I hungered for more. A friend invited me to her non-denominational church, but it was in a small town an hours drive away. I thought there was just no way, but when the pastor where I currently attended unexpectedly stepped down, I thought I might as well take her up on the offer.

My insides were beaming from what was being preached! I immediately knew this was the spiritual food I craved. For the next two years, my brother and I drove that hour to church, and another hour home, once a week, sometimes twice. Unbeknownst to the other, we each got a stirring to move there. I really didn't want to live in a small town again.

I had been counseling with my new pastor for a few months when I told him about my prompting to relocate. He didn't encourage me one way or another. Instead, he gave me a scripture using my life as a metaphor. He said my wandering life was like a tree being constantly uprooted. In order to flourish to my potential, I needed to be planted in one place for my roots to be firmly and deeply established. He said if I moved for God, solely to seek Him and for no other reason than to be planted in His house, allowing my roots to get established in His Word, God would flourish me in the courts of life. I had never heard such a thing, but I was sold-out to the idea that God could do something with a life, in which up to that point, I was failing.

Hebrews 11:1 NIV
Colossians 2:7 AMPC
Ephesians 3:17-19 AMP

For God is not the author of confusion, but of peace...

1 Corinthians 14:33 KJV

May I Have This Dance?

"I'm sitting here, debating whether to go dancing tonight... I really want to go but just thinking about dancing with other men...it doesn't feel right. So I made a commitment within; the next man I dance with will be my husband. But when? I also question whether he is being accountable to me... Lord, I'm really trusting YOU." – Journal Entry, 2009

In an empty apartment, living on my own, I was confused by the sudden indecision I felt about going dancing. Anxiety about making the wrong decision loomed over me. Suddenly, a scripture lighted upon my mind where Jesus ate among the tax collectors – I took that as my "ok" to go out. But I didn't go out that night, nor the next night, nor the following weekend. As my heart became tender to the things of God, the club life I knew and LOVED had come to an end. Did I miss it? Yes. Could I have continued if I wanted to? Yes. Was the opportunity to go out always available? Yes. Did I sense God tell me to stop? No! I *chose* to stop. I wanted to *please* God and, also, honor the man I thought, *surely*, was just around the corner. *"I need you to be blameless, just as he is blameless,"* were the confirming words God spoke to me about my decision.

Since then, I have been to multiple weddings where I sat so worried about having to turn men down if they asked me to dance. I would make myself inaccessible, hiding from view, shielding myself next to my dad and amongst male relatives to keep my promise. Even refusing friends who persisted and insisted that it was nothing more than a dance. Oh the eternity of an awkward minute... A dance would have hurt no one. The temporary attention and affection would have made some lonely moments easier to bear, and not to mention, fun!

But I have kept the vow I made to a God I can't see and to a husband I haven't even met, so when I am in the embrace of that man it will serve as yet another reminder of God's passionate pursuit of my life.

> Hebrews 11:6 NIV
> Psalm 119:1-8 MSG
> Psalm 15:2-5 NIV

*In the morning, O Lord,
You will hear my voice;*

*in the morning
I will prepare a prayer for You*

*and watch
    and wait
        for You to speak*

to my heart.

Psalm 5:3 AMP

Mountain Biking

It was our very first day to ride and my brother was unloading the bikes for us. I was looking into the wooded areas and down the steep hills we would soon embark upon, and just like that an image was dropped into the recesses of my mind. Hands. I immediately recognized them as God's. He was openly extending them towards me, and in them He was holding a heart. I immediately knew whose heart it was – my husband's. I had an overwhelming sense that God was showing me how special this man is to HIM, that He loves him very much. Honestly, my vocabulary is limited as to how to best describe how special this man is in God's eyes.

One would think this amazing download from the heavens into my spirit about my future husband would be enough, but oh no, not for me. I selfishly asked God, "What about me?" Seriously.

It sounds crazy when people talk about how they hear from God. There were times I questioned that ability myself, whether it was truly God speaking or just figments of my imagination grasping at straws, wanting so bad for this faith thing to be real. Yet now, I am confident God does speak to me, often. Not in an audible voice, but through a peace in the very center of my being, or sometimes by dropping thoughts, words, scriptures or images into my mind.

After that moment in the woods, God has continued speaking to me about this man without me even asking or thinking about him. Once, after watching the summer sunset, I made my way towards my vehicle and happened to glance down at my feet, the sweet whisper that day encouraged me that our steps are getting closer.

Jeremiah 1:11-12 NIV
Numbers 23:19 NIV
Luke 2:19 AMPC

The heart is deceitful
　　　　　　　　above all things...

Jeremiah 17:9 NIV

I heard a story once about a minister who, early on in his calling, believed God told him that he would own an airplane. Years went by and nothing happened. One day he heard about a good deal on a plane and thought that, surely, this is what God was talking about. He made the purchase but in the following days, weeks, and months he struggled to pay on that airplane, struggled to maintain the airplane, and struggled to fuel the airplane. When he went complaining to God about the predicament he felt God had put him in, he clearly heard God say to him, "I never told you *that* was the plane." He got rid of that plane just as fast as he could. Not too long after that someone gave him an airplane, debt free. He said that by creating his own "Ishmael" he could have missed out on God's "Israel" planned for him all along.

Have there been chances for me to get into relationships to try to make *something* happen in the past 11 years? Yes. Like the time my ex-boyfriend contacted me, the time a real *hottie* was interested in me, the time a successful business owner hinted at the possibility of lunch, the new good looking guy who showed up at my church, the time I was approached by a handsome guest at a party. During each one of these opportunities I was lonely, I was seeking, I was praying. I could have easily slapped down the God card and said, "This is him," the answer to my prayers.

Here's the deal. I didn't go to God in any one of these instances. I didn't have to go to God. *I* knew. My flesh wanted to go there, and in most of these cases I allowed my mind to wander with the possibility of being pursued by these men. Earlier this year God spoke some reassuring words to me that He never spoke to me before; He said I would know him. How would I know him? By the way God has already been speaking to me about this man. I now recognize that the thoughts about the qualities I would like in a man are God's way of telling me about him, so when the time is right, I will easily recognize him.

Galatians 4:22-23 NIV
Genesis 21:1-2 NIV
Psalm 119:116 NLT

...the One who lifts my head.

Psalm 3:3 NAS

"My resolve seems weakened today. I am experiencing first hand my current group of single friends trying, testing, and pursing relationships. Lord, help me, because I have sensed a twinge of "why them and not me?" Forgive me because that is not who I want to be. I need to be happy for them because one day someone else may be looking at me wondering when it will happen for them. I want to remember the twinge I feel in my heart now and how disappointment tried to set in... And how I, on many different occasions, have had to muster the courage to pick up my downcast soul, look to YOU and encourage myself that one day my time will come, too. I have smiled one too many times behind disappointment, behind tears shed in silence, thanking YOU as I am now, with tears streaming down my face. Thanking YOU, because beneath the hurt and disappointment, there is a confidence that YOU will come through."
– Journal Entry, 2015

When will it happen for me? ...the question that taunts me each time I hear of another relationship blossoming into marriage. As I approached my thirties, I used to keep a tally sheet in the back of my mind of all the school friends who were still unmarried. We were few in number, but at least I was not alone...then. In my mind I still had time and life was full of hope if at least one of them was on this path with me.

The struggle has been real: reading about new relationships on social media, hearing about new relationships from people in town, and as I'm in the midst of new-found friendships, the challenge of keeping my soul in check when it wants to place blame on my current circumstances and pick up a petty offense because it hasn't happened for me as quickly as it has for them. The reasoning, the doubts, and the jealousy that tries to arise, questioning if God has forgotten me or if I have totally missed an opportunity with a guy because I have been too picky.

Yet, when I have exhausted the questioning, all I am left with is the Word: my only comfort, my only peace in turmoil, the only source of strength to continue on this path, even when it looks so bleak to me in times like these.

Psalm 116:4-10 GWT
Deuteronomy 31:8 AMPC
Isaiah 41:10 AMPC

Though it tarry,

wait for it; because

it will surely come...

Habakkuk 2:3 KJV

I am not athletic... never have been. So I don't know why I thought that would change a few years ago when I told a couple of my siblings I was going to join a soccer league. A co-ed soccer league! Never in all my life had I played real soccer, but I went out there determined to make this my sport, my hobby, and perhaps meet an eligible soccer player. At halftime, I informed my brother that I was finished. Done. Playing. Soccer. He scolded, "YOU CAN'T QUIT IN THE MIDDLE OF A GAME!" It was exhausting running up and down, going back and forth! I couldn't keep up with the ball, I didn't know where it was half the time, and not once did that ball even grace my foot. Not once did my teammates pass it to me. I was discouraged, tired, exhausted, frustrated... I wanted to quit!

At different times I have wanted to quit this process, too – showing up to church, reading the Word, speaking the Word, guarding my mouth when it seems like it's just not working and it's taking too long, when it feels like there has been no real manifestation, no real results, no change. I have been discouraged, tired, exhausted, frustrated... and have wanted to quit. The Word of God is filled with instructions for us to see each area of our lives radically transformed. We are encouraged that if we don't quit, we will reap.

What will we reap? Whatever Word of God we are renewing our minds to believe for... *as* we continually show up to church, confess the Word, put it into practice by placing it before our eyes, putting it in our ears, voicing it out of our mouths and into our hearts, and walking it out. In doing so we are activating the power of the Word of God to change our circumstances. We can't quit in the middle of what will be our greatest blessing!

1 Corinthians 9:25-27 AMP
Galatians 6:9 AMPC
Romans 8:22-25 MSG

For the Word that God speaks is alive and full of power, making it active, operative, energizing, and effective...

Hebrews 4:12 AMPC

"Lord, I am so excited about what YOU spoke to my heart! You told me that my future spouse would pursue me and that he would win my heart. I will trust YOUR perfect timing!" – Journal Entry, 2005

This journal entry was written only one year into my faith walk. I remember sitting in the chapel praying from a singles devotional when I heard those sweet words from my God. I was on a spiritual high, which made it easy to tell God I would trust Him. But the harsh reality was that no man pursued me that day, that week, that month or even in the long tumultuous years that would follow.

Truthfully, I forgot those encouraging words spoken to me by my Creator, and the vow I made that day to trust His timing. There was no waiting on God then. I continued in my hot pursuit of guys and relationships. But I was aware that something was missing. Such a deep dissatisfaction now lined the relationships I kept pursing.

After digging up this journal entry, I realize the dissatisfaction was a result of my forgetful impatience with what God had spoken to my heart – those four words I tucked into my journal ten years ago – *he will pursue you*. God in His infinite goodness had marked my heart that day so my spirit could recognize my husband.

Thank God that He is not like we who easily forget… I forgot this word as quickly as He gave it to me. But He didn't forget. Unbeknownst to me, this word became a seed – its roots actively staking claim to its territory; my heart. I left it unattended, but God continued to cultivate it.

Proverbs 15:23 AMPC
Isaiah 55:11 AMPC
Genesis 28:15 AMPC

Listen!

I've told you this before it happens.

Matthew 24:25 GWT

What'd He Say?

In town grocery shopping with my mom one Saturday, I was keenly aware of a tall, young and apparently very handsome man, stalling, in the same aisle. I didn't catch a glimpse of his left hand. When we moved, he moved, and when we met up on the next aisle, I just breezed by him, without making eye contact, in a totally disinterested fashion. Argh! Anyway, he moved on, we moved on, and that was it. I wanted so badly to meet up again, this time would be different; this time I would make eye contact and *smile*. Sometimes my mind and my flesh have me thinking I have missed many an opportunity because I did nothing – nothing to throw the man a bone. But from God there was no prompting, no urging.

On a different day, while sitting in my car, I got a strong sense from God that I needed to be the last of my group to leave the park. I felt God saying I needed to drive by myself, follow the caravan of five vehicles, and pray the entire way home. On the highway, our gas grill flew from the bed of the first vehicle causing debris to fly towards my brother's car behind it. My brother swerved; his quick reaction didn't cause a chain reaction even though his car took a hit from other debris. The rest of us, and our vehicles, were unscathed.

More and more I am realizing that it is not my move. It is God's move to lead me as I calm and quiet my soul to hear the prompting He gives my heart. I simply need to be aware of what God is speaking to me. One day I was just a girl with a heightened awareness of a cute guy on aisle six, and another one on aisle ten, and a few others before I made my way out of the store. On another day, I avoided getting hit by a flying grill on the freeway, or a more devastating outcome, because of my willingness to quickly follow His prompting when I didn't know why. There are no missed opportunities when you are obedient to God's prompting.

Galatians 5:16 AMP
John 16:13 AMPC
John 14:17 NIV

So is the kingdom of God,

as if a man should cast seed into the ground;

and should sleep, and rise night and day,

and the seed should spring and grow up,

he knows not how.

Mark 4:26-27 KJV

"Why does the process take so long? When am I going to start seeing the fruit from all the Word I have been sowing and speaking?" – Journal Entry, 2016

Because, we're all farmers according to the Bible: the *Word* of God is incorruptible seed (1 Peter 1:23), the sower sows *the Word* (Mark 4:14), and the seed is *the Word* of God (Luke 8:11).

Since I was a young girl, my dad has had a garden. He enjoys his garden. He literally spends all day, everyday watching over the seed he has sown. Every year he has jalapenos, cilantro, onions, squash, melon, tomatoes… and a few years back he planted a pecan. Do you know it took years, *years,* before that tree produced anything? Five to seven years at least, but now, that tree produces yearly, and it is the biggest tree in his garden, providing shade for my parents as my dad diligently and vigilantly watches his crops so that the seed he has planted will not be eaten or devoured by pests.

Just like my dad, we are all farmers when we sow the Word of God by speaking it or hearing it, while sitting under the teaching of it, but unlike my dad whose entire days are spent in his garden, we don't have all day to water, cultivate, pull out weeds, and spray for insects. We have lives to live, jobs to work, businesses to grow, families to rear, school to attend… So who is watching over our seed to water, guard, and protect it? The Word of God itself does, if we continue, not just by hearing it and speaking it, but also by being doers of His instructions. As we do, we have the assurance that God is hearing us, the seed – His Word – although not yet seen above ground, its roots are actively digging their way down deep into the ground. In due season, the seed, the things we are believing God for that are based on the promises found *in His Word,* will produce if we don't quit, if we don't grow weary in well doing. At the appointed and set time we will reap those promises, if we don't give up.

I remember a quote I read many years ago when I was just a baby Christian. In an oversized painting, its beautiful foliage left an indelible impression on my life:

"The trees that are slow to grow bear the best fruit…" –Moliere.

Mark 4:1-20 MSG, Isaiah 27:3, Malachi 3:11 AMPC

*But
no human being can tame
the tongue. It is a restless evil,
full of deadly poison.*

James 3:8 NIV

More than once I have wanted to quit this process of waiting. My mind, playing menacing tricks on me, cruelly insists that I have orchestrated this elaborate faith-tale of God, a protagonist and hero, and fabricated a make-believe story of His rescue to hide behind and cope with the reality of this harsh world and my present single circumstances. And tonight my heart feels weakened by the pounding facts overwhelming my mind. It feels like the very depth of my core is bleeding from an unrelenting torment. It is in instances like tonight that I am made aware of the hairline fractures in my once battered heart that have yet to heal in this season of waiting... and I can no longer contain the tears.

In moments like today I want to scream out loud and agree with the masses that perhaps this faith walk is all too make believe. In times like tonight, I want to give my soul relief by speaking forth the evident, providing some form of alleviation from internalizing all these thoughts – thoughts that appear to go unheard unless I voice them out of my mouth. I want to scream and make sure that someone, anyone, is hearing me.

Tonight, I let my mind go where it shouldn't. I've dwelt on my present circumstances of being single, thirty, and there being absolutely no indication that what I am doing is in fact bringing me closer to a husband. Tonight I feel very alone, crushed with self-pity, and so immediately I've begun to question this walk of faith. But even in times of disillusionment like this, there are still things I dare not speak – that this is taking a long, long time – because the power of spoken words once ran rampant in my life creating destruction. Tonight I didn't speak the obvious, truly believing that in doing so I would be pulling up the roots of what's been sown – that even though nothing has surfaced, deep below there is a life its own, gathering strength to breakthrough.

> Numbers 21:4-5 MSG
> James 3:5-6 MSG
> Psalm 141:3 AMP

...yet
I do not know what tomorrow will bring...

James 4:14 ESV

Through the Valley...

"Today I met an amazing woman, thirty-four and single. We really hit it off – she's like me! A dreamer! We spoke about our lives, our dreams and men. I left with a new purpose, a new vision for THE ONE. She really encouraged me to follow my heart – live to the fullest, enjoy being single. She really inspired me." – Journal Entry, 2006

I was in my twenties when I met her. I remember thinking that it could not happen to me – being in my thirties and still single. She was, perhaps, an exception. This woman was beautiful, smart, and successful, drove a luxury vehicle, and lived in a beautiful home! It never occurred to me that one day I, too, would be where she was – in my thirties and still single. She went on to marry a man she felt was the one, and I, well, I have surpassed her both in age and singleness.

As I think back, she pointed out the highlights of being single to me, but left out the dark valleys I would trek through alone. The abject loneliness I would be enveloped in when I had no direction, not even from God. The hurt I felt when it seemed like God could care less that I was still unmarried. The misery and the torment I faced in a room surrounded by couples and I was always, always the loner. Tears shed alone and no one to share them or confide in. The bottomless, empty, and all-consuming pit of self-pity I would try to ease with smiles, the hopeless feelings that left me drained, and the alleviation I sometimes found in sleeping it all away.

It was on these kinds of days I would question my faith, my God; when the solitude seemed insurmountable. But I showed up to church one more time, I pressed play for one more faith CD, I opened my mouth to utter a scripture just one more time… because this, too, shall pass.

I took her advice – I followed Jesus with all my heart.

Psalm 23:4 AMPC
Isaiah 43:2 NLT
Deuteronomy 2:7 AMP

Do not conform

*to the pattern
of this world,*

but be transformed

*by the renewing
of your mind.*

Then you will be able

*to test and approve
what God's will is -*

His good,

*pleasing
and perfect will.*

Romans 12:2 NIV

I felt cheated. I would have had the privilege of kissing those full lips. I would have felt elevated. Important. I would have satisfied the sexual feelings that even to this day I struggle to deny and suppress. I would have someone to catch a movie with, to kiss goodnight, to laugh with, to cry with, to enjoy life with, to dance with, to share holidays with, to confide in and in turn be his confidant. I would have someone's hand to hold, someone to hold me tight and whisper sweet things. I would have cheered him on in his endeavors, his games, his victories, shared his heartaches, reassured his doubts, his insecurities, cured his loneliness... It seemed as if I'd been denied the customary joys of life.

Instead, I simply got time with God. I spent lonely nights, weeks, months and years on my knees, raising my hands to an invisible God I struggled to believe in. I continually blamed God for my obvious shortcomings, and He, without reproach, without judgment, without condemnation for my actions allowed me to yell, kick and scream while tenderly engulfing me in His presence time and time again, and with a still small voice, it was He who encouraged me that, one day, I would rise up to a new and different life. On the darkest of nights His peace pacified me as I uttered Jesus' name, when fear loomed over my bed, gripped my chest, and inundated my mind. When I had no one to confide in, no one to trust in, no one to hold and no one to hold me, I hammered away at my hardened heart, I plowed the fields of my weeded mind with God's Word day in and day out, mining through my once stony heart until I experienced the sweet smell of fertile soil, as if it were crumbling through my hands – and all I could do was fall to my knees in reverent thankfulness, for my labor had not been in vain.

And so I continued digging, and digging, and digging, and eventually I discovered the springs, and then cascades of living water that have given me far more freedom, peace, restoration, and physical healing than could ever have been given by the carnal pursuit of any man.

1 Corinthians 7:17 MSG
1 Corinthians 7:32-35 MSG
Philippians 3:8 AMPC

When the enemy comes in
   like a flood,
  the Spirit of the Lord
   will lift up
    a standard against him...

Isaiah 59:19 KJV

Silencing the Enemy

There is so much noise. The noise in my head reminding me that all my school friends are married; the noise in my heart longing for companionship; the noise from family when I see the look and sense the underlying disappointment that I am not married yet; the noise from acquaintances telling me to do this dating site or try harder to get noticed, the noise from church where it looks like everyone else can just pray and have it happen for them; the noise from the media where we idolize relationships that jump from one relationship into another relationship into another relationship, labeling that the norm of society and everyone else should follow.

There are two enemies using my mind as their battleground. One side stands strong in faith, fueling my belief in what I've heard from God and encouraging me in my walk. The opponent viciously attacks, violating all rules of warfare with the sole mission to steal, kill, and destroy all signs of life. Both sides are in agreement that I am set apart, consecrated territory. Armies of angels barricade me in, defending and protecting my will to be obedient and hold out for God's timing. The opposition orders me to surrender to the way the world does things, aggressively trying to break down my defenses, trying to command my flesh to retreat and make things happen myself before it's too late, or I will always be alone.

Even as I write, I feel the heaviness about the reality of my situation. It seems impossible that God could lead my husband to me here, in a far, far, faraway land in the middle of nowhere (this small town I now live in, best known for its retirement community).

This faith walk has not been without resistance. Sometimes I have questioned whether I would make it through. There are moments it feels overwhelming. Physically, when I have been too drained to fight, and emotionally, to weak to cry, I muster my will to utter these scriptures. His peace floods my soul, and the nagging noise finally relents.

2 Chronicles 32:6-15 MSG
Deuteronomy 20:1-4 NIV
Ephesians 6:10-18 NIV

*...SURELY I AM WITH YOU ALWAYS,
TO THE VERY END...*

Matthew 28:20 NIV

Ni Siquiera Una Sola Hoja se Mueve Sin la Ayuda de Dios
Not Even a Single Leaf Moves Without the Help of God

It is the small things I see on a daily basis that help me look forward to the days ahead. It is when I can lay hands on my physical body and speak to an ailment and it disappears. It is when I walk out the front door and the gate is already open; I see God's hand in the gesture. It is during the day as I am soaking up the sun, or in the evening in my room, and I hear the rustle of the leaves in the wind; I sense it's a way He is attracting my attention and reminding me of His presence. It is when I have had a stressful day and I am able to get on my knees and find a peace that removes all the turmoil of the day. It is when I find favor with people who are impolite on the phone and have abruptly hung up on me, but as I keep my cool, they return the phone call with a (somehow) renewed kindness. It is when I can clearly communicate the thoughts I have and another person is able to understand me completely. It is when I have an event or something important on the calendar coming up and I am gently reminded of it in time… Thank you, Holy Spirit.

A peace that surpasses my understanding now stands guard over my life. It is in the excitement of living each day in a career that just feels like an extension of my life and not a job. When I feel wronged by a person and take an offense, I'm reminded of times where my own actions caused an offense, and that insight gives me mercy and compassion for the other person.

So even though I can't see His face, hear His voice or touch His hand, these constant reminders are a reassurance that He is with me and that I am not alone. When it seems like I have no one to turn to, I can turn to Him. When I don't feel understood, He understands. When this faith walks seems lonely I can speak to Him. I can cling to Him. I can trust Him. I can hope in Him… He is always with me.

John 14:26-27 AMP
Philippians 4:7 AMP
Exodus 33:14 MSG

*The Lord is my Strength
and my impenetrable Shield;*

*my heart trusts in,
relies on
and confidently leans on
Him,
and I am helped.*

Psalm 28:7 AMP

Mind, Will, and Emotions

"Can I really trust YOU? Is it my move YOU'RE waiting on? If so, what does that look like? If not, why do I feel this way? This gnawing feeling I get when I, sometimes, stop and consider exactly where my life is right now. My reality. I've always been so awkward with boys. Perhaps, it's because I am so skinny. Perhaps, men don't find me attractive". – Journal Entry, 2016

Without a doubt, it is my *heart* that trusts in God. The questioning, the doubting, the unbelief comes from my *soul*, which is made up of my mind, my will and my emotions.

My *Mind* – constantly working overtime and mostly dependent on what I feed it: social media, news, movies, or the Word of God. Unrestrained, it conjures images that always play out the worst possible outcomes.

My *Will* – the ability to choose between my way or God's way; going out to see and be seen or staying in to study the Word; to flirt with the cute guy or remain calm; rush onto dating sites or wait on God's timing. And each time I choose the latter (even when I really haven't wanted to) I exercise strength over my will, subsequently making God's way easier to choose each time I face a decision.

My *Emotions* – a pendulum going from one extreme to another in a matter of seconds; hopeful when God speaks to my heart in my quiet times of study to hopeless when I see couples enjoying their love-lives, or when news of another engagement is announced, or magical wedding images are plastered before me.

Then there is my *Heart* – reassuring my soul that I can do this by faith; beating with excitement at what God is doing with my life, what God *has* done, and what God *will* do! That I am on the right path as I continually renew my mind to believe the Word of God. My Heart: wanting to show-off the goodness of God in my life. My Heart, at peace, that at precisely the right moment I will step into the plans God has for my married life as I pursue His plans for the rest of it.

Proverbs 4:23-27 MSG
Psalm 62:5-6 AMPC
Philippians 2:13 AMP

Call unto me,
>and I will answer you,
>>and show you
>great and mighty things...

Jeremiah 33:3 KJV

There is a secret place with my God where mysteries are revealed to me by sweet whispers – a word, a scripture, a thought which lights upon my mind; a result of the investment of time spent praying. I enjoy this communication that happens with God and me. I pray quite often.

Prayer was a foreign concept I found difficult to grasp in the beginning. Did I have to get on my knees, or were there specific words I should say? Should I be doing a combination of both? I didn't really know what prayer was until I heard a simple definition of the term: prayer is simply having a conversation with God. Just talking to God. And sometimes you just sit and listen and wait to see what He will speak to your heart.

So then, how does one know that it is Him speaking? When I joined the prayer group at church, many times I heard nothing, and many times I fell asleep in those early morning hours, until I started sensing that God was giving me scriptures… I didn't initially voice them out, but then He got my attention when others would voice the exact scripture He gave me. Through the investment of the Word read, heard, and studied is how He speaks to me. I was beginning to fine-tune His voice, and he was confirming that I could hear from Him, even using other people when I didn't speak up.

I have desires that have not yet come to pass, but still, a statement I find myself saying frequently is, "Life is so exciting!" Because it is true and I believe it. There's an excitement that bubbles up within the very core of my being, excitement about the superabundant quantity and the superior quality of life God created me to have; his good, good plans that continually unfold before me as he is guiding my path and establishing my ways. It is my spirit through which He answers me and reveals the great and mighty things he will do in my life. As you become familiar with His Word, the Holy Spirit will lead you to the scriptures to confirm what He speaks to your heart.

Jeremiah 29:12 AMP
Colossians 4:2 AMPC
2 Timothy 3:16-17 AMP

*Now
Faith is the substance
of things hoped for
the evidence of things
not yet seen.*

Hebrews 11:1 KJV

My siblings and I recruited our younger brother to be our trainer for a new hard-core home workout program. He was an exceptionally tough drill sergeant, watching form and not once allowing us to slow down or quit. This particular summer day was hot, so we moved our workout sessions to the garage. Each day for a couple of weeks I sensed in my gut that, for me, it was not a good idea to be jumping or working out on the hard concrete floor. I voiced my concerns to my brother, but he dismissed it as an excuse for me to get out of working out. So I continued.

Getting out of bed a few weeks after that initial workout session, I realized I couldn't put any weight on my right leg. There was an excruciating pain in my knee. I couldn't even walk on it. Using my good leg, I hopped into the dining room with my Bible when no one was watching. As I sat and read through a few accounts where Jesus healed people, something rose up on the inside of me, and right then I determined that if God could do it for them, He would do it for me. I hopped back into my room (unnoticed) and with those scriptures I painfully attempted to walk around the perimeter of my bed, placing all my weight on my fisted hand to help me move along side the mattress, only slightly touching the floor with the ball of my foot at first. I did this for hours, placing a little more weight on that foot until I could finally put the full weight of my body on it. I had read *the Word*, and I believed it for myself as I voiced it out of my mouth repeatedly, even though fear filled my mind about what further damage I could be causing. I continued… around the bed… declaring God's Word… and the pain lessened until it finally went away.

And so the journey goes… with His Word I continue lining the perimeter of my heart in prayer, strengthening it to believe, fully persuaded by what He has spoken to my heart and what has been confirmed in the pages of the Bible.

Matthew 8:13 KJV
2 Corinthians 4:13-18 NIV
Romans 4 MSG

Thou shalt love the Lord thy God

    with all   thy heart,
and with all   thy soul,
and with all   thy strength,
and with all   thy mind...

Thou shalt love thy neighbor

        as thyself.

Luke 10:27 KJV

"Lord, how can I love someone like I love myself when at times I dislike the very person I am? I feel so inadequate when things don't turn out the way I think they should... I question myself when faced with decisions. I even question my ability in Your things, in this very faith walk, when the results of prayer and petitions and desires are long-waiting... Attitudes arise when I don't get my way. I hate not being able to open up to people. Secretly, I judge individuals sometimes... How could I possibly love my neighbor, a husband, when at times I don't love me? Will I measure my husband against these same attitudes and standards that I have towards myself? Lord, on my own I can not do it – on my own I don't have the patience, I don't have the love – I don't have the motivation, I don't have will power to love someone unconditionally when I don't love me. Lord, help me to change. Change me." – Journal Entry, 2016

It's not a coincidence that God asks us to love Him first. In doing so, we experience, firsthand, the grace that He extends us in our brokenness. In our lowest, darkest places there is no condemnation, no blame; only compassion, pity, understanding, forgiveness, sympathy, and as we experience the freedom that can only be offered through Jesus, it enables us to love ourselves, and in turn, others.

In God's eyes I am made perfect by of the blood of Jesus, yet I often forget to look at others through those same eyes. I am harder on myself, and others, than God will ever be. I cannot properly love someone if I don't love me, and I can't properly love me if I don't love God.

John 13:34 NIV
1 Peter 4:8 AMPC
1 John 4:7-21 NIV

Only, let each one live the life which the Lord has assigned him, and to which God has called him.

1 Corinthians 7:17 AMP

Third Time's a Charm

Single, living a city of over 1 million people, unable to find men to date, I decided to see what all the hype was about with online dating. I carefully created my profile, exaggerating qualities (such as my income and highest level of education) and only listing my positive attributes. Then I waited, impatiently checking the app for matches or someone to reach out to me. I got ZERO matches. I got zero takers. No one was interested.

A *decade* later, I tried it again. I completed an exhaustive profile, this time answering the questions as honestly as I could, all the while thinking – *what am I doing?* But I dismissed the voice in my head because I had matches! About ten, instantly! There was an unemployed guy, a bus driver, two bald guys, all of them seemed uneducated and way past the prime of their lives… From my shallow, superficial, judgmental perspective I couldn't bring myself to converse with a single one, so I instantly deleted my profile to avoid them ever contacting me.

My final attempt to online date was when I heard of the app where you simply swipe. I must have gotten the name of the app wrong because apparently the way to a woman's heart was by the size of a man's private parts. That's what the profile pictures consisted of… oh, and shortly thereafter, my email inbox was inundated by more of the same.

I know numerous people, including close friends, who have had success with online dating. Some even got married! I am in no way opposed to it. At different times I have even gone to God just to check if He has changed His mind about *me* doing it. But He has not given me the green light to do it: His peace. He had already spoken to my heart about me recognizing the one when the time is right. That He would be my matchmaker.

1 Corinthians 7:17 AMP
Romans 8:24-25 AMPC
Philippians 3:12-14 MSG

Beware lest you say in your heart, 'My power and the might of my hand have gotten me this...'

Deuteronomy 8:17 ESV

"I will trust Your perfect timing." – Journal Entry, 2005

I don't jump into relationships anymore. As a matter of fact, I don't jump into dates anymore either, but I can say, as a single woman, my antennae are always up, always aware of men in my age range who aren't sporting a wedding band. Without a doubt, I have toyed with the possibility of what it would look like if I facilitated more dating by *encouraging* single guys who I find attractive to go out for coffee or a seemly innocent lunch date. My reasoning mind tries to convince me that I need to put myself out there, date around, so that maybe, just maybe, *my efforts* would reveal that one of those men were put on my path by God in response to my prayers. If it's going to be, it's up to me, right?

In my entire dating career, only three guys actually pursued me first. With all the others, *I* was timing it, calculating my moves, "accidently" running into the object of my affection. I was the one conniving to make things happen with men.

We may know *exactly* what we want when it comes to our men and think these clueless boys "need encouragement". Otherwise, we would have to wait forever. But we are not called to play God by orchestrating the outcome we want, or play the part of man. Actions, or the lack thereof, are telling signs. They point to deeper issues that will ultimately shape the relationship and no doubt serve as a reflection of what can be expected in that relationship and in a guy's character...his maturity level, his confidence, his motivation to go after what he wants, his drive to do whatever it takes... or *maybe* he's just not interested.

I have had to cut off the desperate noise in my head to avoid falling victim to how I used to operate, reminding myself...

If he didn't pursue – it's not my responsibility to do so.
If he didn't ask – it's not my job to do so.
If he didn't call – it's not up to me to make something happen.

1 Peter 2:11 AMPC
Proverbs 3:5-7 MSG
Song of Solomon 8:4 ISV

*And I saw heaven opened, and behold a white horse;
and he that sat upon him was called Faithful and True...*

Revelation 19:11 KJV

I enjoy a good romantic movie – those are my absolute favorite. Many times I've imagined myself in the role of the lead female. A few years ago, I watched a drama intertwining three love stories. They did an exceptional job casting good-looking men as the leads. And the movie portrayed these men EXACTLY how I have many times envisioned my man to act, be, and treat me! Every quality I secretly fantasized - the zealous hero, physically strong, an uncompromising integrity, the perfect gentleman, an intelligent leader, a passionate lover, a devoted husband, adoring partner, and avid provider. It was a compelling movie I didn't want to end.

So enthralled, I made it my personal mission to find out all I could about the lead male actors. Surely, they had cast these perfect men because their lives best reflected the roles they portrayed. But I was so naïve – their lives were anything but stellar, besides the fact that all had failed marriages and relationships. This shattered my distorted view of reality. Even more disappointingly, I found out it was a movie written by a *woman*. A woman, who, like me, held an unrealistic view of what a perfect man was to be. Numerous movies, like this one, watched over my lifetime, framed my mindset, distorted my expectations, and as a result, I was placing unrealistic standards on men. Standards where love was defined by romance and uncontrolled emotion… when romance and emotion should be the result of love.

Love, true love, is defined by the Word of God. It is modeled by the One in whose image we were created. Love, true love, is patient, kind, does not envy, does not boast, is not proud, does not dishonor others, is not self-seeking, is not easily angered. Always protects, always trusts, always hopes, and always perseveres. Love, true love, never fails.

James 1:16-18 MSG
1 Corinthians 13:4-8 AMPC
1 Corinthians 13:13 AMP

Wait on the Lord:

be of good courage,

and He shall strengthen your heart:

wait, I say,

                          on The Lord.

Psalm 27:14 KJV

Giddy-up!

I took horseback riding lessons this week for the first time. I've spent this summer kayaking my local rivers. I am learning a new language. I got involved with Toastmasters last month. Since June, I have had a personal trainer. These last two years I have traveled more than in all my thirty years combined. I am glad to be doing all these things now, because at one point I was in a state of *waiting*. Waiting to do new things because I had no one to share these experiences. I felt stuck.

I was waiting to live and experience life because I felt that new experiences would be meaningless and insignificant without a husband. I had no desire to pursue other hopes and dreams. My ultimate dream was my husband. He was the end all. He was the goal. He was my answer. He was my god. Finding him was the answer to all life issues. I was setting myself up for failure. I had no vision past the wedding day. I had no plans for children. It was just him and me, and somehow my world revolved around him. Life would be good when I found him. I had high expectations of him, but he would be fine with my mediocre life.

Not once did God ask me to wait to experience life or tell me I wasn't allowed to enjoy myself. The waiting He has asked me to do is about attending and adhering to the Word, to uncover His thoughts, plans, and purposes for my whole life, not just a season of it. I am no longer scratching the surface of unsettled desires but allowing God to reveal His well thought out plans, His ability to do exceedingly abundantly beyond my greatest hopes and dreams; plans for my single-hood that will serve as stepping stones into eternity, not just married life. The waiting process is not about me *not* doing *anything* – it is the process of my soul being untwisted and rewound around the truth of God's Word, so the Holy Spirit can continually repair, fortify, restrain, and strengthen it, for me to emerge as the victor I was created to be.

I am experiencing new things not just so that I have more to offer this man when our lives unite, but so that God can use me to the fullest extent of His design for my life.

Proverbs 31:10 AMP
Proverbs 31:17 AMP
Proverbs 31:25 AMP

*See to it, then,
that the light within you
is not darkness...*

Luke 11:35 NIV

There is always a sliver of hope when the prospect of meeting a single man is imminent. This one in particular was visiting town with his mother, staying the week at my B&B above our salon. My mind went wild playing out all the endless possibilities. Perhaps this is the moment I have been anxiously awaiting. The one. My overactive mind already reading too much into the situation before I'd even laid eyes on him… the winking emoji as he bade me good night via text the first night.

The next morning our paths momentarily crossed at a distance from in our vehicles: only friendly waves exchanged. Later, he reportedly stopped in to drop off a bag of cookies; I missed him, again. At the end of the day we finally made our official introduction. Our hands clasped as our eyes locked, and he held a strong grip, shifting all his personal belongings onto his left arm, concealing his left hand from view. I casually invited him in to tour the building, as I tend to do with most guests. Small talk ensued before he excused himself to his mother waiting upstairs.

The following day our paths did not cross once. Too bad: I had selected my wardrobe for a possible encounter. So I checked up on him via text message to "make sure his accommodations were satisfactory." He informed me he would be by the salon the next day to chat. When he did come in, his eyes were clearly fixed on me among all the other women in the salon, *me*, and he greeted me with a compliment, "You look nice." He rested his arms across his chest and it was in that moment that his wedding band reflected in the mirror he stood near. Disappointment swept over me.

During my quiet time with God in the hours leading up to our meeting, I sensed those words in my spirit; *he is not the one*. I chose to ignore them, allowing my mind to entertain erotic thoughts laced in lust and longing. For the rest of his stay my mind was confused as to the attentiveness of this man towards me, and him not mentioning his wife… and then I was reminded of those five words in the midst of my disappointment, not in condemnation, but as a reminder that God does tell us of things to come.

1 John 2:16 AMP
1 Corinthians 3:3 NLT
Ephesians 4:22-23 NASB

*For you were once darkness,
but now you are light in the Lord.
Live as children of light*

Ephesians 5:8 NIV

I could never understand why a single woman would want to seek the affections of a married man, until that exact temptation almost swept me in. There was something beautiful about his display of willingness to help me. And I was nice because, truthfully, at times I have been nicer to strangers than those closest to me. Perhaps in his vulnerability he found a girl who was willing to listen; I didn't judge him, I didn't question him, I didn't challenge him. I just gave him what I needed at the time: companionship and a listening ear. In my mind, I was making excuses for both our behaviors. And when I was faced with his invitation for dinner, I was tempted to say yes… yes to a man who was married.

The first time I put myself in a position like this was during college. At the end of a Tejano concert, a security guard invited my friends and I – out of hundreds of other women – onto the tour bus. The two vocalists were clearly married, but they were famous, which made up for their looks and justified our flirtatious behavior. The lead singer, prompted and teased by his band mates to talk to me, actually wanted nothing to do with me. At the time, being rejected, even by a married man, was a blow to my ego. I still wanted to be the object of his desire, to hold the upper hand, to be the one doing the rejecting. I was seeking a man's attention, his approval. Even then, I knew that marriage boundaries should not be crossed, but I naively believed that, because they were famous, nothing bad would happen to us girls on a bus outnumbered by older men.

I don't know what would have happened that day if he had been interested in me. I, like my friend, could have been picked for one of them to do with me as he pleased, all because I said yes to an invitation to hang out. The expectations always seem to be different with men. Nevertheless, I always found stories of adultery repugnant, but the wanting of attention and approval overrode my own judgment, and there I was at the crossroads of having to make a decision that involved a married man.

Hebrews 13:4 AMP
James 1:13-15 NIV
Genesis 4:7 AMP

Then when the illicit desire has conceived, it gives birth to sin;

and when sin has run its course, it gives birth to death.

James 1:15 AMP

He was kind, attentive, and not bad looking. It felt so good having a man's attention, and the details were extremely charming. Each day the anticipation of seeing him toyed with my mind. His flattering words left a lingering impression. The look in his eyes aroused a desire in the pit of my stomach. I let my mind go there before I realized he was married, and when I realized he was married, it still went there against my better judgment. I felt and saw how easily this temptation could overtake my soul – it clouded my mind and deceived me. Who was I to ask about his wife if *he* didn't bring her up?

The night before this B&B guest departed, he invited my sister and me to dinner. Compelled to honor a prior commitment, I declined his invitation. Had I not *already* had plans, I may have gone. The internal struggle to cancel my existing plans to be in the company of a man who lavished me with attention and admiration was overwhelming. My reasoning mind was trying to convince me that this would be nothing more than an innocent dinner with a married man to talk as friends. It wouldn't go beyond that *because I know my limits, I am a strong woman of God, and I desire to please God.* As I drove away, the invitation was luring me to go back… if only for a moment my soul could be satisfied with the presence of a man I felt connected to, and who found me attractive. As I drove away, I looked back one final time in hopes of catching the last glimpse of a man I knew I would never see again. I was already committing an act I know is wrong: craving the attention of a married man.

You don't *happen* to find yourself in sin. It all starts in the mind first. Thoughts seem innocent in the confinement of the mind, but if you continue to rehearse and replay lustful thoughts you will eventually find yourself playing out those actions. What images are you continually feeding your soul? As my pastor says, "…you can't think a thought away." You change your thoughts by SPEAKING, and by speaking the Word, you guard your heart and your mind.

        James 4:17 AMP
        Mark 7:20-23 AMP
        Proverbs 4:23 NIV

Do not merely listen to the word, and so deceive yourselves.

Do what it says.

James 1:22 NIV

"I felt something, someone, missing today. I felt alone today. I didn't much enjoy today. I know YOU have someone, Lord. I missed him today". – Journal Entry, 2010

What does the Word say? In recent years, it is a phrase that I have coined for myself when faced with a difficult situation. As I read through some of my old journal entries, it's interesting to find how my feelings were in direct opposition to the word of God. What a distorted life I lived without the Word.

Today in my life I don't feel like "he" is missing or that my life is broken because I am still unwed. Those feelings, that once consumed me, have left. They are replaced with peace from God's Word. No longer are my days filled with an all-consuming distortion that my purpose in life, my ultimate hope and only goal, was in finding myself a man. I was busy comparing my life to others I wanted to emulate, not realizing that my hope and wholeness was in the pages of God's Word.

As I continued pursuing God, He started putting the broken pieces of my life back together; my thinking, my body, my true purpose. I believe that God is ever ready to take us to a deeper level, a more meaningful relationship, a heightened understanding and awareness of Him. But it is our carnal desires and the getting of our own way where we must surrender if we are to obtain such peace. The struggle to satisfy our flesh, to appease its natural appetite for pleasure, must be controlled. It is in pursuit of God's presence and guidance that we obtain the peace we were created to walk in daily – nothing missing, nothing broken.

Peace cannot rest on what I heard preached once, scriptures I can quote, or Bible stories I can narrate back. My peace is cemented as I speak the Word of God out of my mouth, put it in my heart, and before my eyes *continually*.

2 Timothy 3:14-17 MSG
John 8:31-32 KJV
Luke 11:28 AMP

So will My word be
    which goes forth from My mouth;
It will not return to Me empty,
    Without accomplishing what I desire,
And without succeeding
    in the matter for which I sent it.

Isaiah 55:11 NAS

I got them as a Christmas gift, my first pair of brand-name sunglasses. I never paid more than ten bucks for sunglasses. Later that year, I walked into church and laid them down along with my keys. When I walked out that day, I couldn't locate them. I knew I took them in. Immediately, my first declaration was that, in the name of Jesus, I would find them. The investment of the word I had been feeding my soul over the last ten years is what first flooded my mind and rushed out of my mouth. One week later I still had not located them. I looked in the lost and found, I looked under my car seats, I continued asking the people I saw earlier in the week, retracing my steps, refusing to believe or speak that they were lost. And with each passing week I got discouraged, eventually purchasing another pair of ten-dollar sunglasses. But I kept the lost pair's case on my dashboard as a reminder that I would get them back.

The last week in December, I gave up. The words finally made it out of my mouth; my new sunglasses were lost. There. I felt like I had sealed the deal of never seeing them again because I said it. This whole time I had been proclaiming such belief, really believing, and just like that it was over. But it wasn't…

From time to time we may doubt, we may even throw in the towel or give in to our flesh. Is that ok? No, not really. And we know that. But here is the deal… each time we repent and change our course and take one more step in the right direction, God is faithful to His Word. That first day I gave Him my faith by returning the very thing he gave me: His Word. I believed it and He was watching over the very words I spoke to perform them. We may not get an immediate answer in the hours, days, weeks, or even months that follow, and the discouragement is real. But when we get what we've asked for against all odds, there is only one explanation for it, and then it strengthens our faith to believe for the next thing.

…three months from the time my new sunglasses had gone missing, on January 1st, they appeared in the lost and found.

Philippians 4:6 NLT
James 3:2 NLT
2 Timothy 2:13 NIV

Love not the world, neither the things that are in the world.

1 John 2:15 KJV

All the things I believed would be remedied in my life and made complete by finding myself a man (my joy, my wholeness, my peace, my purpose) were the very things that I needed from God. But the notion that God would want anything to do with my romantic relationships was ridiculous, out of His scope; not a part of his job description, especially given the intimate nature of these relationships. He was just a Father, and that would be weird. As a follower of Christ, my understanding of how intimately God wants to be involved in my love life has become clear.

God created the very institution of marriage. God; the *Creator*. Man, love, and marriage are His *creation*. Yet, we go around loving the creation more – many times excluding or even denying the Creator. The idea given to me by creation was that success in life would be determined and measured by when I got an education, got married, lived in a house with a white picket-fence, had kids while working forty-plus hours a week, then retiring. No mention of God. In my mind, I just needed to check off the boxes. There was nothing deeper. Any education, any house, any career… and any man would do.

But what if… what *if* we were created to do more in our marriages than just buy the house with the white picket-fence, *become* more in our marriages by understanding the power of two becoming one? What if, in fact, God is challenging us to do away with the status quo, as we seek Him, the *Creator*, first, and then trust *Him* for our greatest love story?

What if the stirring in your heart is telling you to hold off, to wait, to delay the immediate gratification of finding a mate, of pursuing creation, to first understand who you really are, what you were created for, and how God cares about you first, as single, before you are to be part of a marriage? God wants to be involved, so you can step into the career, the marriage, the house, the life *He* created you to have.

Colossians 1:16-17 NIV
Ephesians 2:10 NIV
Matthew 6:30-33 MSG

*...all my days
were written in Your book and planned
before a single one of them began.*

Psalm 139:16 HCSB

The Book of Life

Every moment, every opportunity, every second is not about finding the one. It used to be. Every trip I took, every corner I rounded, every person I met, every step I took I was secretly wishing that this one thing I am doing will place me face to face with the one. And on each New Year, my resolve was the same — that THIS would be my last holiday alone, without a man. So *I kissed dating goodbye*, I tried discovering *the secret* to attracting my husband from across the universe, I exhausted the *five love languages* whenever *boy meets girl*, endlessly trekking the literary forest to uncover the one who was created to be *wild at heart*, to help him understand *how to love me*.

Everyone's story is different. God has made each one of our stories unique. When a person shares their victories, it should serve as an encouragement, as a testament to what God is able to do with another willing heart. I don't want to emulate another person's life — no matter how great it is — I want to be able to hear from God about *me*, about *my* life.

My encouragement to you... there is only one human being that can change your life. JESUS CHRIST. My life changed because of the One and only WORD OF GOD. My life changed when I started breaking down the scriptures and voicing them out of my mouth, so they became revelation and not just words. That is where the true transformation comes.

There is a book God has written of my life unfolding before me. Will I continue turning the pages so I can carry out each day as it is written, even if it doesn't make sense the first time I read it? My heart is open to correction. My life is open to His instruction. He knows best. Without Him, this life would not be worth living. Without Him, I don't know how to live this life to the capacity for which I am created.

John 1:1-4 NIV
Joshua 1:8 NLT
Deuteronomy 32:47 NLT

<u>One</u> – single by union, undivided, the same

<u>Proposal</u> – the act of presenting a plan or suggestion to a group of people; the act of asking someone to marry you

But whoever
is united with The Lord
is One with Him...
1 Corinthians 6:17 NIV

...that they may all be One,
just as you, Father, are in me,
and I in you,
that they also may be in us...
John 17:21 ESV

Two are better than One...
Ecclesiastes 4:8-12 AMPC

...and they shall become One flesh.
Genesis 2:24 AMPC

One – because most all want to find the one. Ideally, we want to get married just one time. And this is just one life touched by the willingness to honor God where romantic relationships are concerned. This is an encouragement and a testament to what happens when one person believes in the power of God in her life.

Proposal – because before I started writing this book, that is what my sole purpose in life revolved around. What can I do to make God see that I am ready for marriage and get *someone* to ask me to marry him? But in the process of writing, he presented a different proposal: His plan. His infinite wisdom showed me all the amazing things I missed when I was only consumed with being found by the one. His plan included me digging deep beneath the layers of my raging desire to be married, finding that He was the One that my entire being was calling out for... and each step of the way, He was there.

One Proposal – because in order to find the one, we first need to know *the* One who created us, and understand who we are as One in Christ; becoming whole, first, as your own person. Then one can fully understand how to fulfill our destiny with another one.

This editing process took twice as long as it took to write the original manuscript, and much of those writings didn't make the cut. In my early writings, I was legalistic in my approach with men, and I was holding on to things that God never spoke to me. God had given me the instruction to write, but in my mind, I blew those instructions out of proportion and predetermined that I was going to get my husband by the time I was done writing. I still had much to learn. Actually, I still have much to learn. My editor, who became a voice of reason and a confidant, challenged me on some of the writings as we approached the end asking, "Are we still *there*, or have we grown since we started this process?" And in researching these very scriptures I knew, I saw them in a different light. As I approach my book release date, I am still on this journey alongside you.

DID YOU ENJOY THE BOOK?

DO YOU WANT TO GO DEEPER?

TAKE THE NEXT STEP TODAY WHILE YOU WAIT
ON THE ONE TO MARRY…

For more information & additional resources get connected with Dalia
at www.daliafranco.com.

CPSIA information can be obtained
at www.ICGtesting.com
Printed in the USA
LVOW10*0135160617
538286LV00005B/6/P